FORMING CHARACTER IN ADOLESCENTS

Originally titled
Character Education in Adolescence

RUDOLF ALLERS, M.D., PH.D.

Roman Catholic Books
A Division of Catholic Media Apostolate
Distribution Center: Post Office Box 2286, Fort Collins, CO 80522

Nihil Obstat

✠ Most Rev. Francis J. Spellman, D.D., LL.D.

Archbishop of New York

Imprimatur

Arthur J. Scanlan, S.T.D.

Censor Librorum

Originally published in 1940

ISBN 0-912141-67-0

TABLE OF CONTENTS

Rudolf Allers, M.D., Ph.D. — and husband & father

After a distinguished teaching career in Europe earlier this century — and 7 years of service on the Ecclesiastical Court — the extraordinary Dr. Rudolf Allers came to America. Married and a father, he taught for years at Catholic University in Washington, and wrote half a dozen books and scores of articles. Several of the leading Catholic publications of the day endorsed *Self Improvement*, and heaped praise on his other books as well.

INTRODUCTION

So MANY BOOKS are written to-day on education and its psychological foundations that a new work seems to stand in need of justification. It must have things to say that are not said in the books already existing; or it must say in a new and more impressive manner things frequently discussed; or finally it must offer a new technique or a new philosophy of education. If it does none of these things, it is apparently useless.

The author of the present little book has to confess that he does not venture to claim for it any of the justifications mentioned. What he has to say is not new; the facts he shall refer to are well known; he cannot even aspire to the distinction of telling them in a new and more impressive manner; he has no new philosophy to offer. But he feels, curiously enough, that these very circumstances which apparently ought to dissuade him from publishing these pages, entitle him to submit his ideas to the reader.

If the facts presented in this book are not new but rather obvious, they are nevertheless usually misstated to-day. Too many prejudices of all kinds influence the minds of contemporary writers on education, with the result that they have become incapable of seeing the simple and obvious facts as they are. Thus, the point of view from which the considerations in the following chapters are developed, is not new at all; but the considerations may be justly called unusual — at least in comparison with the average writings on this topic that one encounters to-day. Nor is our philosophy new; it is neither progressive nor modern in the usual sense. But it is, if not modern, at least factual and indeed very much so, and this is something far better and more important than modernity.

The one feature of this work which may claim, up to a certain degree, to be new is the combination of the old and well-known facts with the equally, even much more, old but not well enough known philosophy. This indeed is the very aim and meaning of this book: to view the facts in the light of this old philosophy and to explain the principles of this philosophy as the very best means of interpreting the facts.

This book, then, deals with character education in adolescence. It desires to be mainly and in an eminent degree practical. It renounces, therefore, all extended discussion of the basic psychological and philosophical notions it uses. These things have been alluded to — though still not so thoroughly as a truly philosophical discussion demands — by the author elsewhere, in so far as psychology has to be considered; and the philosophical truths and principles underlying this work may be found in any manual of Catholic philosophy.

Because of this desire to be eminently practical, the author has tried to eliminate as far as possible all technicalities, whether of psychology or of philosophy. Furthermore, lest he should tire the reader, he has abstained from quoting articles on psychology or philosophical treatises. Whoever desires to become acquainted with the original data of psychological research, may turn to one of the many textbooks on educational psychology or on child-development. It is, however, necessary to caution the guile-less reader against one danger. When perusing such works or articles, he will encounter statements which are said to be based on "facts," and which contradict flatly certain basic points of view defended in this book, or certain principles held to be true by the philosophy on which this book rests. There is, of course, the possibility of the present author being wrong; to deny this possibility would be silly. But such contradictions may be also viewed from another aspect. What is described as a "fact" by many modern psychologists is not seldom much more than a simple fact, if by this term we understand, as we ought, the simple and unprejudiced description of findings or observations. What is called a fact by modern writers, is but too often a finding couched in the language of some theory; though the authors say, and even believe, that they are going to prove their theory by the fact they re-port, it is very often the case that they view the findings in the light of their theory of whose truth they are con-vinced beforehand.

This influence of preconceived theories becomes par-ticularly great and disastrous whenever the facts, or what are called by this name, are used to prove or endorse certain practical measures. Whole systems of education have been based on preconceived theories, though the founders believed them to be based on facts.

There can be but little doubt, if any, about simple facts. An observable fact can be rediscovered by anyone after it has been discovered once. There is, accordingly, but little altercation over mere facts; new facts may be doubted because they contradict certain beliefs or theories, but if the facts are confirmed by further observations, there is no argument which can disprove them. But theories, explanations, and practical conclusions are always, and rightly, open to discussion.

Theories must explain all the facts known about a certain group of things or events; whenever new facts are established, the theory has either to prove itself capable of explaining them, or it must be modified, and may be eventually abandoned. But man has a tendency to cling to explanations once accepted; because of a certain conservatism or species of inertia characteristic of human nature, or for other reasons, he is generally unwilling to give up ideas. He will then rather try to fit the facts to the theory, even at the risk of doing some violence to the facts. This conservative attitude is, however, not as bad as some ultramodern and excessively "progressive" people will have it to be; it may preserve us from subscribing to unfounded ideas which may be received enthusiastically to-day and discarded to-morrow. The inclination consciously or (as is the rule) unconsciously to bend facts to make them fit with a cherished theory is, however, very bad indeed.

The haste with which certain minds jump at the newest and most modern theory would cause but little harm, if the attitude adopted were merely theoretical. But it causes the "reformers" to start immediately some practical reform, for instance, in education. These people usually say that the new facts force us to change our practical measures and to adopt others more in accordance with the alleged facts. Very often, however, it is general ideas and not facts which gain the greatest influence. A practical measure is never the consequence of mere facts or of pure science. Facts tell us only what is, and the theories of science try to state why it is thus. Practice, however, means applying a knowledge of facts and theories to certain ends. All practical measures, whether taken by an engineer in building a bridge, or by an inspector of police in striving to maintain order, or by a teacher who wishes his pupils to learn things, or by a physician who tries to help a sick person to regain health — all practical measures taken by these and other people are adopted for the sake of realizing certain aims. And it is the nature of the aims which dictates the kind of measures these people take. The engineer knows how to build a bridge, but he has to be told where a bridge is needed and for what — a railroad, heavy cars, or just pedestrians. The inspector of police knows the measures necessary to preserve order, but why order has to be kept is something which is entirely outside his province; order must be kept because the community or the higher authorities wish it. The teacher uses the didactic methods in vogue, because he himself has been told that knowledge is desirable and necessary, and the physician knows that man desires to be freed from suffering and to be given back health; that these are aims approved by man in general is nothing which could be deduced from the information supplied in the textbooks on teaching or on medicine.

Every practical measure, then, is determined by the ends

which it is applied to realize. Educational measures, in particular, depend on what is believed to be the true aim of education. Science is absolutely and essentially incapable of discovering anything about aims. If someone tells us that we have to pursue this or that aim because of some statements of science, we may be sure beforehand that he is wrong; he may, of course, be right in recommending certain aims, but he is right, not because of his appeal to science, but in spite of it.

We are taught what is right and what is wrong, not by science, but by morals or by moral philosophy. Anyone pretending that science, whether biology or psychology or sociology, is capable of stating anything regarding aims, has either not grasped the true nature of morals and other normative disciplines and has misunderstood the essence and the limitations of science, or he is fettered by some prejudices which are themselves, not of a scientific, but of a philosophical nature.

Some people, if they are told that their ideas (for instance, on education) are due to their cherishing some definite philosophical views, will retort rather angrily that this is not the case, nor can it be the case, since they have neither a philosophy nor do they believe in such. Philosophy is to them mere speculation — an at least unnecessary, and probably even harmful, occupation for idle minds. They, the reformers, are practical, unswayed by speculation, absolutely matter-of-fact, and so on. But they do not see that passing a judgment on philosophy and its importance for humanity is itself an act of philosophy. If a man says: "Philosophy is nonsense, because only science has a real value," he makes a statement which science is incapable of proving or disproving. Science does not know anything of values. The deadliest poison is just a chemical substance to the chemist; he is quite indifferent to any use of this compound; the laws of ballistics are the same for a rope thrown to a man in danger of being drowned and for a shell fired by an eighteen-inch gun. It is not science which tells us whether to use a rope for hanging a man or for helping him out of a pit into which he has fallen. Nor does science forbid poisoning our enemy.

All the talk about how science and its advances teach us what aims to pursue in education or in politics or in what not, is, to state it bluntly, pure nonsense. It is never science which tells us what is good and what not, though there are many scientists who believe themselves entitled to render such judgment. If they are entitled, they are surely so, not because of their science, but because of some other reasons. A knowledge of atoms does not enable one to know what is good and right for man. Nobody is an authority on social reform or on education, because he knows all that can be known about the brain of a rabbit.

It is, therefore, doubtful whether the invasion by science of the field of education has been of much profit to the latter, or whether it has not, upon the whole, done more harm than good. We do not attempt here to decide this question finally. However, everyone should know that science can tell us only of methods to use for the realization of aims; the aims we have to discover elsewhere.

The very common mistake of overrating or rather misjudging altogether the true nature of science causes many people to state as facts what are in truth facts dressed up in the terms of some special theory or philosophy. This is the reason why people sometimes feel quite startled by so-called "facts" which apparently contradict truths they know to be immutable. But must one not accept facts! Many a man indeed has been greatly distressed by the belief that the "facts" of modern science and his old convictions were incompatible; he was unwilling to give up his convictions which rested, as he knew, on very solid, on eternal, foundations, but he could not but be disturbed at the thought that science, this much-adored idol of modern times, contradicted his faith.

If this man — and there have been and still are many of his kind — understood better the nature of science and of so-called facts, and if he had a clearer idea of the nature of philosophy or faith, he would never have been the victim of worry. He would have known that he need not worry at all, because science can never make any statement regarding the deepest principles of being or regarding the ultimate aims of human striving.

Once one has come to reflect on these things, one really wonders why they are not generally recognized; much trouble and much discussion would be avoided if these truths were known and realized in wider circles.

The facts that will be mentioned in the following pages are just mere and naked facts. They do not, as such, contradict any essential truth or any basic law of morals. Maybe they contradict some time-honored ideas; certainly they are going to contradict some of the modern views on education and on the nature of the adolescent — and, for that matter, of the adult mind too. Holding an old conviction is, of course, as little a guarantee of the possession of truth as is admiration for one of the newest and most modern ideas. Yet, surely there is quite as much chance that a view held for centuries is true, as one published in the last issue of an ultra-modern educational magazine.

All these things have to be asserted, and very plainly too. There are but too many persons who are easily impressed by the latest discovery of science and who are quite incapable of forming an opinion of their own. They just swallow everything that is presented to them as the newest progress of science (mostly, not by scientific journals, but by digests or by some magazine).

Though science has proved itself incapable of fulfilling all the promises the nineteenth century so credulously accepted, and though to the critical eye the bankruptcy of science as a reliable basis for erecting the edifice of a happy and satisfactory life has become but too visible, there are still many who preserve carefully the mentality of the eighties and the nineties of the last century, and who believe themselves to be modern, enlightened and progressive, whereas they are in truth obscurantists, behind their time, and the greatest obstacles to real progress.

It may be wrong to look back and to praise unreservedly the good old times: they were indeed better times in many a respect, even though there were no radio, no planes, and generally speaking none of the great improvements we are so proud of to-day. However, it is just as wrong to make an idol of the latest idea.

This book hopes to prove that the knowledge of facts which we owe to the research-work of modern times is not only compatible but in full accordance with ideas which are quite old, indeed nearly two thousand years old.

Scientific research in the field of general psychology, of the psychology of mental development, of character and character formation has brought to light many interesting and important facts. These facts, however, are but confirmations of ideas which have been alive in mankind quite a long time. If this identity has not been fully recognized as yet, it is because of two reasons: the psychologists are not acquainted with those writings in which these ideas have been expressed, and the philosophers, and Catholics in general, feel a little suspicious when they are told of the recent advances of science and especially of psychology. This attitude is not quite unjustified, since so many new "truths" prove to be rather short-lived, and since the statement of facts is so often mixed up with pseudo-philosophical ideas or with theories on human nature which cannot but meet rejection.

There are, however, some people even among Catholics who feel that we ought to take up every proposal whatsoever and make use of every discovery whatsoever, if we want to be "up-to-date"; they fear that by not being "progressive" they run the risk of being left behind and losing the race. This fear is quite unfounded. Modernity is something very changeable; what is modern to-day is obsolete to-morrow. The chance of permanent validity is much greater for ideas which already have been frequently put to the test.

Notwithstanding all this caution, we must be grateful to modern psychology for having discovered — or in some cases rediscovered — certain truths which are indeed of the greatest importance in education. Perhaps the most beneficent result of the still growing interest in psychology is that our attention has been directed towards certain facts which had been rather overlooked in the past.

This book, then, sees its task in bringing together, as it were, the reliable statements of psychology and the immutable principles of sound philosophy. Its subject is adolescence. But it will be necessary to go back sometimes into childhood, because there are features in adolescent behavior which cannot be understood unless one knows something of their antecedents and their history.

Dealing mainly with education, this book considers psychology only in so far as facts and theories become influential in forming character. Because character-formation is the topic of these pages, other problems of education or training are mentioned only incidentally when and in so far as they have some bearing on the main question.[1]

Most of the ideas proposed here have, in a brief manner, been stated in a series of six articles published in *The Homiletic and Pastoral Review* from October, 1938, to March, 1939. The present writer has to thank the editor and the publisher of the said *Review* for allowing him to reproduce here some passages.

---

[1]Perhaps the writer may be permitted to refer, for more detailed information, to his books: *Psychology of Character* (Sheed & Ward), *Sex-Psychology in Education* (Herder), and *Self-Improvement* (Benziger Brothers).

CHAPTER I

The General Psychology of Adolescence

THE CHILD GROWING from the age of unconsciousness into a gradually enlarging awareness of reality becomes successively acquainted with an infinite number of facts and of things; all of them are absolutely new, never experienced before. The child has to discover reality. That this tremendous task does not terrify the child, and this enormous burden does not break down his still undeveloped forces, is due to his emerging only slowly from unconsciousness and to his getting into touch with reality without being aware of it. When the mind of the child has developed so far that a certain reflection on the self and on his relations to reality becomes possible, most of the things and facts and events have come to be taken for granted; they are the natural and necessary facts, the facts that were always there, the things that, in so far as memory reaches, were always around. This is at least the situation in a normal and average case. It is known that unexpected and far-reaching changes may have a definite influence on the mental development. But for the ends pursued in these pages it is only the normal situation which has to be considered.

In normal cases, then, mental and personal development proceeds rather smoothly. There are indeed periods of crisis, sudden arrests of development, difficulties arising in connection with the individual's fitting into society, or associated with the adjusting of the egotistical self-assertion to the demands of common life. There may be difficulties, too, which are conditioned by certain inner laws of development or by nearly inevitable mistakes made in education or equally inevitable unfavorable influences coming from without. But these conflicts and difficulties are, as a rule, not too serious, and are easily overcome.

Thus, a child at the age of six years or so feels quite at home in the surrounding world. There are no troubling problems; he has come to know most everyday things, at least in a general manner; but very few startling experiences occur. There are, of course, some important changes in the environmental world. Another child is born; one undergoes the quite novel experience of being the older child, of not being any longer the center upon which all the care and all the interest of the family are focussed. New people appear in the field of experience and others disappear; one sees new places, one discovers some previously unknown facts. But all this leaves the personality itself untouched, because there is no true consciousness of personality or of ego in these years. The child, of course, knows himself to be different from others, to be an individual. But this knowledge is an implicit one; it is not clearly defined, and it is hardly ever made a subject of reflection or of analysis.

This happy state of mind persists even during the first years at school. Going to school, having work to do, meeting other children, being subjected to the authority of an unknown person, the teacher, all these are again new experiences, but they are not really troubling. If preschool education has not been too unreasonable, the child had become acquainted with the idea of work already before entering school; the desire for work and for creation is part of the natural outfit of man, and needs but little encouragement and understanding to develop in quite a desirable manner. A child in good physical and mental health becomes soon adjusted to the new situation of school.

A child of six, seven or eight years may ask many questions, but he has no problems in the strict sense of the word. He asks questions because of his natural curiosity, because of his wish to know things and to know his way among them. But his finding a way and his having a place among things and persons is no problem, because he himself is no problem. He takes himself for granted, as he takes the rest of reality. Only rather exceptional conditions may cause him to wonder and to become conscious of having problems; but these moments usually pass rather quickly. Though one never knows for sure what lasting impressions may result, there is generally no immediate effect to be noticed. If a lasting impression has been made, it will, as a rule, manifest itself only in later years. It is indeed a mistake to believe that no harm has been done, because there is no immediate reaction; the effects may appear many years later.

In the years before the onset of adolescence, the child relies in many senses on others. He may possess a quite well-developed tendency towards self-assertion and even self-will, but there are still many things he expects his parents to do; he knows that they will decide for him, and he is in a way glad that they do decide, even though he may not seldom resent his having to obey. His relying, consciously or unconsciously, on his parents and on other environmental persons gives the child a feeling of security which compensates for his objective and subjective inferiority. This inferiority results from the child's awareness of his being relatively helpless, his being small and weak, his still not knowing many things, his encountering so frequently an invincible opposition thwarting the realization of his own purposes. The average situation of childhood is indeed of a kind to engender a definite idea of inferiority; but this idea will not necessarily have unfavorable consequences, if an understanding and sensible education takes care to strengthen the natural and indispensable feeling of self-value.

Having reached the age of six to eight years, the child may feel quite secure and be capable of dealing with new situations. These new situations come normally exclusively from without. The problems the child encounters are of reality and objectivity; the subjective side of experience is as yet almost unnoticed.

All this situation changes, gradually or suddenly as the case may be, with the onset of adolescence. This period is essentially one of trouble and of problems. Accordingly, it is essentially a period of unrest and of uncertainty. The reliability of things and of persons vanishes, not because these things and persons have become different, but because the adolescent's relation to them changes. This change of relation is due to the change in the individual himself, or rather in the consciousness he has of himself.

The naïve attitude which the child had towards himself — his taking himself, his existence, his life and its conditions for granted — all this unproblematic being in harmony with all and each disappears. It is as if the child, when passing from childhood to adolescence, has to rediscover the whole world, and this task is definitely more difficult than the original discovery, because it has become conscious. The happy unconsciousness of early childhood is lost forever.

This task, quite sufficiently difficult in itself, is rendered still more difficult by the fact that one's environment changes continuously. The world presents an ever-changing aspect; it is no longer the same to-day as it was yesterday. This indeed very troubling fact is due, of course, to the rapid changes going on in and with the adolescent's personality. It is he who changes, and whose point of view becomes every day, so to say, another. But changing one's point of view means seeing things under an equally changing perspective, discovering always new features and witnessing other features sliding back into invisibility.

Nobody can ever hope to understand the adolescent mind, and even less to influence it somewhat, unless he is fully aware of the fact that uncertainty is the very basic feature of this age.

Seen from without, adolescence is the period of transition between childhood and adult life. Every period of transition partakes as well of the past as of the future. Adolescence presents itself accordingly as a curious mixture of features characteristic of childhood and of others, still undeveloped and but just indicated, of adult mentality. But the infantile features are no longer quite the same as they were but a short time before, and the adult characteristics are not as yet what they will be after a couple of years. The former do not correspond any more with the essence of the adolescent personality; they give therefore often the impression, not of being childlike, but of being childish. They persist, so to say, because those which are destined to replace them are not ripe; but they no longer fit the adolescent completely; there is a certain discrepancy between the personality one senses beneath the adolescent behavior and this behavior itself. This discrepancy is felt also, though only dimly, by the adolescent himself, and contributes to increasing his uncertainty. But he cannot as yet get rid of these habits and ideas, because there are none which could replace them.

The adolescent is more or less clearly aware of the fact that his old habits and ways of thought, those he felt to be suited to himself only a short time before, are no longer adequate to his present state; but he does not know enough of this state to become aware of what is really amiss with these views. He feels himself change, he envisions some-how that he is becoming different, and he knows, of course, of the result of this development; but his idea of adult mentality is abstracted from his experience with others, and he cannot apply this rather theoretical knowl-edge to his own personality. The adolescent is perhaps not able to find a precise expression for his state of mind, be-cause everything is vague and uncertain; but he would doubtless, if he were capable of such an analysis, have to say: "I know what being an adult is and how it looks, but

I have no idea of how it feels." That is, he cannot translate, as it were, his theoretical knowledge into an anticipation of personal experience. This, be it said incidentally, does not contradict the well-known fact that children are sometimes amazingly sharp-sighted and capable of understanding others, even adults.

The adolescent does not know what is the matter with him; he does not know himself, and accordingly feels at a loss in the face of reality and its problems. This ignorance becomes still more accentuated by the continuous changes which go on in the adolescent's mind. Though he does not know for sure what it is that changes, he is acutely aware of the changes as such. His will to find something he can rely upon is thwarted by the elusiveness of his self; one might indeed try to find out about an unknown thing, and hope that patient endeavor will be crowned by success, but the task becomes hopeless if the unknown thing itself never remains the same and presents every day new and startling features. Such exactly is the case in this instance. The adolescent is never sure, so to say, that he will be tomorrow morning the same as he is this evening when he falls into sleep. Things may become utterly different overnight. What was lovable to-day may be detestable to-morrow. Things which seemed devoid of all interest may be enthralling the next day. Projects which were conceived enthusiastically may become stale and stupid within twenty-four hours.

Something begins to develop within the adolescent's personality which urges him to rely on himself, to give up the habit of appealing to others and of trusting them for dealing with every difficulty; but at the same time there is nothing to rely upon but this ever-changing, ever-elusive, ever-mysterious self.

The formation and solidification of the self is the very essence of the developmental processes during adolescence. Even though the child knows himself to be a self or an ego and never confuses his own person with any object whatsoever, he lives merged in the surrounding world; he moves in this world securely and with a definite knowledge of this world's laws and properties. This at least is the case with the normal child, after the first years of gradually becoming acquainted with reality have passed away. But the child does not consciously differentiate himself from reality; he does not feel forced to take and maintain a personal attitude towards the world. His having but an undeveloped self and his knowing not much of himself, therefore, does not become a reason for worry and for self-analysis. It is, however, a basic characteristic of the mature mind that it stands not only within reality, but at the same time opposed to it.

It is obvious that many troubles which plague man, to-day perhaps even more than ever, result from his incapacity to maintain the right mean between these two equally fundamental features of his nature, viz., his being in and at the same time opposed to reality, belonging to it as one of its parts and having it, on the other hand, opposed as an object. This essentially human situation assumes a still more serious aspect in the case of the adolescent, since in his mind there is no clarity either as to the nature of the necessary attitudes, or as to what takes such attitudes, the self.

The formation of the definite self is the central phenomenon and the real problem of adolescence. All other features and factors that we observe during this period of development are either but aspects of this one central process or secondary to it.

One can never hope to attain a real understanding of the adolescent mind, unless one fully acknowledges the central and fundamental importance of this process of formation and consolidation of the self. The subjective mirroring of this process is *uncertainty,* which accordingly becomes the very characteristic of adolescence.

To emphasize this point is all the more important since a common opinion still holds the awakening of sexuality to be the central fact in adolescence. This idea has indeed been abandoned by a good many of the leading psychologists; but it continues to be believed by most people, whether parents, teachers, or educators. Nobody will, of course, deny that the arising of sexual desires plays a great rôle in adolescence. The bodily transformation associated with the maturing of sexuality — the development of what biology calls the secondary sexual features — cannot be overlooked, nor can we ignore the fact that sexuality conditions many new and unwonted experiences. Nevertheless, the view which makes sexual development the very center of adolescence is mistaken.

There are several reasons why this idea is so generally accepted. First, the phenomena of sexual awakening are rather striking, objectively as well as from the standpoint of subjective experience. Sexual things hold quite often a prominent place in the thoughts of young people. Sexual maturity manifests itself by noticeable bodily changes, and therefore becomes more visible than the subtler and more hidden mental processes. But the fact that a phenomenon is more remarkable, does not prove it to be the essential thing in a complex of others. Symptoms which are very impressive to the superficial and unsophisticated observer may reveal nothing of the true nature of a disease; the very same symptoms may even be absent, and the disease of which they are believed to be the most important manifestation may nevertheless exist. This is, for instance, the case with epilepsy; it is generally believed that the epileptic attack or paroxysm is the disease itself, but the psychiatrist knows that there are cases of undoubted epilepsy in which the paroxysms may be missing altogether.

The natural temptation to identify what is impressive with what is essential is one of the reasons why sexuality has been considered to be the very basis of adolescent development.

Another reason is probably a certain tradition which connects sexual maturity with the attainment of manhood. Among primitive races as well as some of a higher culture, sexual maturity is regarded as a sign of general maturity being attained; there are rites of initiation, of conferring the rights and duties of citizenship, etc., in which sexual factors are very prominent. But this does not prove that, even in the mind of these races, sexuality is more than but one manifestation of maturity, one which can be easily ascertained and which therefore is used as a criterion for deciding on maturity.

But there are other rites of initiation, too, which do not

take any account at all of sexual maturity. Whether sexual maturity had been reached or not was not asked in the initiation to knighthood; the important point was whether the squire had done deeds of valor, whether he had shown himself reliable and courteous, whether his life had been ruled by the laws of chivalry.

The fact that there exist non-sexual rites of initiation ought to be sufficient for disproving the idea of maturity meaning essentially and always sexual ripeness. The sexological conception would probably not have met with so much applause from modern authors if it had not been in accordance with the general materialistic trend of the nineteenth century. Materialism, in abandoning the notion of a spiritual soul as distinct from matter, was forced to find explanations for every mental phenomenon. Mind and its operations came to be considered as a mere manifestation of brain-processes or, generally speaking, of bodily alterations. The tendency to regard physiology as the very basis of all science of human nature grew so strong that even scholars who were not true materialists succumbed to the allurement. The famous theory of emotions devised by William James is a striking instance thereof: "We do not weep because we are sad, but we are sad because we weep." James was not what one would call a materialist. But his theory of emotions is definitely expressive of a materialistic spirit. In the nineteenth century scientific explanations had to be materialistic.

The very moment the essence of human nature is seen in the body and its functions, adolescence very easily comes to be interpreted as consisting mainly in sexual development, because the various bodily changes going on in this age are indeed closely related to sexual development. We know that an arrest of the latter may condition a retardation of all the other changes belonging to puberty.

There are, however, some very impressive facts which discountenance altogether this theory. One of these facts is that sexual and mental adolescence may become separated from each other. There are individuals whose bodily and sexual development progressed regularly, but who nevertheless remained mentally on the level of pre-adolescence. We do not, of course, allude to feeble-mindedness; the cases we have in mind are of quite normal persons. Nor does the statement of a retardation of mental development imply any kind of intellectual backwardness; the individuals in question may be even very intelligent and efficient. What remains undeveloped is not reason or intellect, but character and the full consciousness of the self. In such cases one observes a second "crisis of puberty," often several years after sexual maturity has been reached, in which crisis, serious though it often is, sexuality does not play any rôle.

A conscientious analysis of facts in normal adolescence and the observation of such cases as have been just alluded to show apparently that sexuality is but one side or factor among others, and that it does not constitute the very essence of adolescence.

It has been said also that the essential feature of adolescence is the individual's becoming conscious of his belonging to this sex or to that one. The authors who hold this opinion do not mean, of course, to imply that a child may not and does not know itself to be a boy or a girl. What they wish to convey is the idea that in adolescence the full consciousness of what it means to belong to one of these sexes first dawns on the mind and gradually acquires full clarity. This is doubtless true as long as it is taken as a mere description of what is going on in adolescence. But it is very doubtful whether this process is to be considered as the very essence of the changes which occur during adolescence.

To develop this full and clear consciousness of belonging to one of the sexes, and accordingly to know of the peculiar position allotted to the individual in the world, especially in the world of society, presupposes a clear and full consciousness of self. One has to be first, so to say, a self before one can be a man or a woman. The arising of the first-mentioned consciousness is but a consequence and a more special determination of the consciousness of being a self. Being a man or woman defines somehow certain tasks and positions among one's fellows. It means moreover a particular specification of the general idea of being a self. It may be quite impossible to define and to describe the differences obtaining between the manner in which a man and a woman know of their respective selves; but there is little doubt of there existing peculiarities of self-consciousness in both sexes. But these are nuances, varieties of the general and common self-consciousness which belongs to human nature. The awareness of one's belonging to one of the sexes is therefore the result and a further determination of the general self-consciousness. The problem of the relations to the other sex is similarly only a special case of the general problem of the relations to others; sexual relations are indeed a special case of social relations.

It seems furthermore that by making self-development, in the sense indicated above, and its subjective correlative of uncertainty the fundamental features of adolescence, one arrives at a much better understanding and a much more uniform idea of the nature of this troublesome age. The following remarks will, we hope, make this clear.

A normal child in the pre-adolescent years has generally a well-defined character, because it has quite precise, if unexpressed, ideas on the world and the aims one might pursue therein. The adolescent has, so to say, no character, or rather the essential point is that his character impresses the observer as not deserving this name. This impression is caused particularly by the instability of behavior which is so characteristic of many adolescents, and with which, quite unjustly, they are very often reproached. This reproach is intelligible in so far as the instability of behavior is disconcerting to other people, because one cannot rely on the promises an adolescent makes, because one does not know how to deal with him; but an intelligible attitude is not necessarily an intelligent one. The adolescent indeed is not guilty of, or at least not responsible for, the inconstancy of his behavior. It is an inevitable result of his state.

Some psychologists, making use of the terms coined by typology, speak of an alternation of "introverted" and "extraverted" phases. Introversion means that the center of gravity is, so to say, in the interior of personality, that the interests concentrate mainly on subjective experiences, that to the external world a lesser importance is accorded than to the world of feelings, of dreams, and of imaginations. The introverted personality is, accordingly, rather unsocial, disinclined to take part in reality, not interested in work and things; he lives apparently in a kind of splendid isolation, within a world of his own. To him fully applies the saying of Heraclitus of Ephesus: "They who are awake have all one world in common; the dreamer has a world all by himself alone." The extraverted is just the opposite of the first type, living more in surrounding reality than within his own personality, caring but little for what goes on in the interior of his self, captivated by everything going on around him. Extraversion is, be it said incidentally, no guarantee for stability of interest and of work. A person may be so much extraverted that everything affects him, every new impression fascinates him just as long as it is new; he may neglect his own personality so completely that he even becomes forgetful of all sense of duty. Extreme extraversion is as abnormal as is extreme introversion.

This last description of adolescence is acceptable as a reference to certain of its quite obvious sides. But it does not go deep enough to supply a satisfactory and comprehensive theory. It is deficient especially because it deals only with a formal side of mentality. Introversion and extraversion are formal ways of making one side or the other the aim of interest or attention; but these terms in themselves tell us nothing regarding what sides or features of reality interest the extravert, or what peculiar phenomena of inner life enthrall the mind of the introvert.

Extraversion prevails in a normal and healthy child. Though even such a child may sometimes and for short periods lapse into dreaming and forget reality, becoming wrapped up in an imaginary world, the average attitude is one of interest in things, in persons, in facts, in the world in general. He may become absorbed by dreams as he does by games; but a child who forgets everything around him because only the game exists for his mind is not introverted. Playing is an activity which deals with reality; it becomes an escape from reality only much later in life. A grown-up man, or even a child of some ten or twelve years, may play for the sake of forgetting reality; the younger child lives in reality even when playing, perhaps even particularly then.

Extraversion is indeed so characteristic of the normal infantile mentality that some have argued that only extraverted personalities are capable of teaching and educating children. This is, of course, an exaggeration due to a certain overrating of the importance of types. To teach or to educate successfully one ought to be a well-balanced personality — one whose interest is divided, according to objective needs, between the interior and the exterior world. A person whose mind is of a pure extraverted type is as unsuited for education as one who is wholly wrapped up in himself. Neither of the two is capable of understanding another's personality.

The appearance of phases of introversion is very often the first intimation to the older people of the changes going on in the child. The withdrawal from reality, manifesting itself as introversion, is something they were not accustomed to observe in the child. It is necessary to grasp the full meaning of and the reasons for this withdrawal.

A retreat from reality is caused very often either because the individual feels scared by reality or because he has suffered defeat. Man withdraws generally from dangers or from obstacles he cannot overcome. The natural reaction to a situation which is sensed as perilous is flight; the natural consequence of our becoming aware of insurmountable obstacles is capitulation. These reactions ensue, in the life of the adult, when certain partial situations arise which condition such an awareness of danger or of unsuccess. But the world in general is the place wherein the normal adult mind feels at home; it is his world, the one which he knows and which he has partly fashioned himself. The adolescent mind, however, has to face a world as yet unknown, one in which he is precisely not at home, which is in a way strange and uncanny; and he has to face it while he is still ignorant of his own forces and capacities. No wonder if he is easily discouraged and takes to flight, withdrawing into the shell of his inner life.

On the other hand, there is a definite attraction in the unknown. If there were no such attraction, humanity would never have progressed beyond primitivity. All advances in science and in technique, all discoveries and inventions, are due to this attraction which the unknown exercises on the human mind. The subjective correlative is, of course, curiosity, which is not always a bad quality, for there is a necessary and justifiable curiosity too. Curiosity is very much alive in the adolescent mind. Scared though he may be, the adolescent is at the same time attracted by the unknown, within himself and without. But this attraction and the desire to know are coupled with the fear caused by the unknown, which is all the stronger since the weapon or the tool by which man hopes to conquer the unknown — that is, his own personality — is itself as yet unknown and untested in its reliability.

It is, therefore, but natural that the basic quality of adolescent mentality is uncertainty. And it is obvious that the interplay of attraction and repulsion, of curiosity and fear, condition these oscillations between introversion and extraversion which contribute so much to making the minds of young people appear fickle and unstable and unreliable.

The essential uncertainty, depending on the very nature of the developmental process, is often increased very markedly by the clumsiness of education. There are to-day two extreme views on education. The one holds that education has been practised quite successfully throughout the thousands of years since man came to exist, and that every man is gifted, in the necessary degree, with the talent of educating his or other people's children. The other view believes education to be terrifically complicated and wishes to rely exclusively on science, especially on psychology and the technique of training and guiding children. Both views are wrong, but the second is perhaps more faulty than the first. Science, as we were told already by Aristotle, deals with generalities; but we have to educate individuals, human individuals in whom individuality is, so to say, more individual than in any other individual we know. We may trust in generalities when we have to apply a law of physics to some particular problem dealing with inanimate mat-

ter; we may rely even on biology and physiology when dealing with a bodily trouble, because matter, dead and living,
is individualized in a lesser degree than is the human person. A stone falling down is an instance or a manifestation
of the law of gravitation; a bodily disease is a "case" (e.g.)
of gastritis; but a human person is not a "case" of humanity. The human person is in a quite peculiar manner unique;
while cases and instances repeat themselves, persons exist
but once. Science being concerned necessarily with generalities, therefore, becomes a rather precarious help to those
who deal with human persons.

This is not tantamount to denying the value of psychology and of the science of education. These are indeed helpful, if they are used in the right manner and within their
limits. What we wish to convey is a warning against an undue and exaggerated "scientification" of education.

The first attitude towards the task of education, the one
which trusts in the natural gifts of man, is right in so far as
man is indeed gifted with the capacity of understanding
another person. We shall not and cannot here discuss the
very arduous problem of the psychological foundations of
this capacity. It exists, and nobody in truth has ever doubted
its existence. The misfortune, however, is that in so many
people this original capacity becomes dulled and, as it were,
blinded by prejudices, by egotisms, by mistaken ideas, and
these factors are the more influential and dangerous, the
less the individual is aware of them. Its service in unmask-
ing these prejudices, in destroying wrong attitudes, and
in correcting mistakes, constitutes the greatest achievement
of science in education. We do not speak here of course of

technical means for presenting certain subjects to the infantile mind (for teaching reading or writing, for making the child understand the meaning of a map, etc.). Education is spoken of here only as the task of forming moral personality and character.

The dawning consciousness of self, and connected therewith the still vague but nevertheless very impressive awareness of being a person, makes the adolescent feel that he ought to rely on himself, that he ought to be independent in his decisions, that he ought to become fully responsible for his actions. From this arises the longing for independence, the tendency for self-assertion, the unwillingness to listen to advice and the repugnance to blind obedience.

The progressive evolution within the mind and the changing outlook on reality which results are quite sufficient to alter the adolescent's attitude towards the objective world, including his relations to people and so also to the parents. The unquestioning confidence which the child had in the wisdom, omniscience, and omnipotence of the parents vanishes quickly. It is indeed necessary that the infantile attitudes be replaced by such as are adequate to the new stage of development. But this replacement is often hampered by a lack of understanding on the side of the parents. They do not notice, and very often are loath to discover, that their child is no longer the little helpless and implicitly trusting being he was but a few months before. They are shocked at seeing the charming traits of childhood disappear, at their child not turning any more to them with the wonted trust and tenderness; and instead of adjusting themselves to the new situation, instead of trying to understand the new budding personality, they reproach the child for things he should not be held responsible for; or they try to treat him as if he were still a little child, whether because they do not know any better, or because they are unwilling to give up the peculiar joy they derived from the helplessness, the confidence, the charm of the playing and gambolling child.

What this situation demands ought to have been done long before. The parents should have followed carefully the gradual, at first almost imperceptible, changes in their child, and adjusted their attitude and their educational measures to them. They should have avoided all behavior which undermined the original trusting love of the child. Unfortunately, parents do many things which somehow estrange their child; these ways of behavior may have no immediate affect, but the impressions go on rankling in some secret place of the child's mind, and they become influential the very moment the inner conditions are of a kind to make confidence difficult, obedience loathsome, and tenderness repulsive.

It is indeed almost impossible to confide in another, be it a beloved parent, if one does not know what to confide. The adolescent may feel, at certain moments, a strong desire for confession, for enlightenment, for consolation; but he neither knows what to confide, nor whereupon to seek enlightenment, nor what really ails him. And even if he has some vague idea of what is the matter with him, he does not know how to express it, for all his experiences are unwonted, new, and different from what he knew before.

The dim feeling of being responsible for himself, the troubles arising in his mind, the new ideas and emotions which he somehow believes to be wrong and which nevertheless impose themselves with an irresistible force, make him moreover ashamed and embarrassed; these states of mind are known to inhibit very much an even definite impulse for speaking out. But there is also another side to the reticence and the embarrassment of adolescents. With the slowly growing consciousness of being a self — absolutely distinct from every other self, having to live its own life and to bear the whole responsibility for its being and doing — the adolescent mind develops a natural reluctance to disclose itself. What makes the parents who were accustomed to the openmindedness of the child (though children have their secrets too, more of them often than the parents suspect) call the adolescent reticent, secretive, and impenetrable, is in truth the first manifestation of a normal and even necessary quality of the adult mind. One may give to this quality the name of discretion, if this word is understood in its original sense (such as it possesses, for instance, in the Rule of St. Benedict), implying the right discernment of things to be told and things to be withheld. Wrong though a general secretiveness and unwillingness to disclose anything of one's inner life under whatsoever conditions is, the habit of pouring out one's feelings, disclosing without any "discretion" one's thoughts, throwing open indiscriminately the windows of the "secret places of the heart," is not less bad. The adolescent, because of his essential uncertainty, does not as yet know how to steer a middle course. He accordingly presents a vacillating behavior; he may be very outspoken one day, and become utterly reticent the next. For this reason it is well to make use of every opportunity he offers to us for becoming acquainted with him and his problems; it will not do, with adolescents, to postpone a discussion, because we never can be sure that to-morrow he will be as willing to confide and to listen as he is to-day.

Since he does not know what to say and how to say it, and does not feel sure that the things he would like to say will be received as he wants them to be, the adolescent easily develops an exaggerated secretiveness. Another reason for this behavior is that he very naturally overrates the singularity and newness of his personal experiences, and therefore feels that nobody is capable of understanding him. This belief is often strengthened by the indeed clumsy behavior of parents and older people in general. But we shall have to say more about this later.

This state of uncertainty is at the bottom of what is so often alluded to as the fickleness of adolescents. They are fickle, no doubt; their interests change rapidly; they form friendships which do not last; they get enthusiastic about things which bore them soon afterwards; they are meek to-day and stubborn to-morrow, willing to work for a short spell and soon disgusted by everything resembling work; at one time they are friendly, considerate, accessible, and then again gruff, egotistic, impossible to approach. All these and many similar things are true. But all the changing moods, all the difficulties created by them, all the trouble at school and at home, are but the externals of the inner uncertainty.

They form friendships because they are in need of someone to cling to, and they abandon their friends because these
prove to be incapable of supplying the security for which
they long. They are willing, inclined to work, friendly,
tractable, as long as the turmoil in their interior subsides a
little, but they become aggressive, lazy, shut up within
themselves whenever the uncertainty becomes more pro-
nounced.

The picture drawn here of the general character of adolescence is erroneous in two senses. First, it is a generalization, and therefore does not apply to any individual. No
individual is ever the representative of the fullness of his
species; only all the individuals taken together give the
species. No wonder then that the individual adolescent
differs in many ways from the description given here. And
the picture is also inaccurate because it does not take into
account the modifying influences of environment and other
forces. Adolescence may develop in a much milder manner.

There is, however, still another point in which this picture may appear as rather remote from reality. In perusing
the description of adolescence and noting the single features enumerated, the reader might get the impression that
adolescence is essentially a period of unhappiness. This is
true in a way. There is more worry and more unhappiness
in adolescence than is generally assumed. But to call adolescence simply a time of unhappiness would be as wrong as
to consider childhood as a period of unbroken bliss. There
is quite a lot of pain and of worry and of unhappiness
even in childhood. But children live mainly in the present,
and most of their painful experiences are soon forgotten,

though neither so completely nor so lastingly as many believe. The glory of happiness which in the eyes of the adults
surrounds childhood is mainly the effect of an illusion of
retrospection, due mostly to the fact that the adult esteems
the lack of responsibility, which indeed is characteristic of
childhood, to be an enormous asset. As a whole, one might
indeed well call childhood a happy age, especially because
of its peculiar attitude towards time. The future means but
little, if anything at all, to children; and the past vanishes
quickly, because the present fills up the child's mind. One
would be, however, mistaken if one should in a similar
manner think of adolescence as an age which, as a whole,
is one of unhappiness. There is enough reason for being
unhappy, but there are compensations too. For the adolescent mind the future has a definite meaning. Though this
future is but dimly envisioned, and though it quite often
takes on a rather terrifying aspect, there is the consciousness of outgrowing all this and the prospect of becoming before long master of one's own life. There is,
furthermore, the enthralling feeling of novelty, the fascination of the newly discovered self, the awakening awareness of one's capacities, the consciousness of a still increasing strength, the urge of bodily activity to give way to which
becomes a source of definite pleasure, the knowledge that
one is allowed or will be before long allowed things which
were denied to the child and because of which one used to
envy the older people — all these and many similar things
counterbalance somehow the unpleasantness of uncertainty
and the manifold troubles, inner and outer, in which adolescents become so easily involved.

One could, of course, go on indefinitely pointing out single features of the adolescent mind and showing how these are related to the basic fact of uncertainty. We shall have, however, to refer repeatedly to facts of psychology in the following discussions, and may therefore content ourselves here with the things which have been said.

Chapter II

Ways of Understanding and Approach

KNOWING ALL, in a general way, of the psychology of adolescence does not as yet enable us to deal with an individual case. General or theoretical knowledge and practice are different things, very much different indeed. Many a man has known perfectly the general facts, and has nevertheless proved incapable of understanding a particular individual. A witty philosopher once said that it is very easy to understand women, but impossible to understand a woman; this is true in a certain sense of every human being, and in a particular way of young people.

The need of individual understanding is even greater in the case of the adolescent than in that of children. There is no other way to gain influence over a person than by means of understanding; if you do not know what kind of material you have in your hands, you never can fashion it. It has always been remarked that the problem of authority is one of the greatest in the education of adolescents; it becomes so great because of the difficulties of understanding the adolescent subjected to authority.

Authority is already a problem in the training of children; but as long as the original bond of loving trust persists between parent and child, the task of influencing children is not too arduous. Authority is a problem with adults too; but they may be willing to submit to lawful

38

authority or to that of experience, because their reason tells them that this is the thing to do. But adolescence is no longer inclined to rely on others. The growing knowledge of being a person in one's own rights causes authority to be doubted; the consciousness of increasing strength makes the young mind long for independence. And the adolescent has not as yet gained sufficient insight to be capable of understanding the necessity and the right of authority. Laws appear to him as willful restrictions imposed by the tyranny of the older people; authority is held to be the illegitimate claim of those who possess it for retaining a position which they in truth ought to abdicate. The feeling that the age of the older generation is passing away and that of youth beginning is very common with these adolescents.

No age, therefore, is more difficult to approach and to manage than adolescence; nowhere is the educator, accordingly, more in need of a thorough understanding of the personality he has to direct and to mould.

Understanding means, in the most literal sense of the word, standing under another — that is, bearing his burden and taking his place, sharing therefore his point of view. The fact of having given birth to this expression is a definite tribute to the psychological insight of the nordic languages; "understanding" and the corresponding words in German, Dutch, etc., express the real situation much better than does the Latin *comprehendere* and its derivatives. To understand the adolescent mind, we have to become perfectly aware of the way it conceives itself and reality, so as to share completely its point of view.

The main feature of the adolescent mind is, as has been pointed out in the foregoing chapter, uncertainty. To understand the situation of youth, its peculiar perspective, and to put oneself in its place, one has to realize what it means to be uncertain and how the world looks to a person who has fallen into the clutches of uncertainty. Perhaps the great and still growing uncertainty of these our days has something to do with the often remarked fact that there is a kind of "juvenilism" in the general mentality, a persistence in the minds of many an adult person of features which in truth belong to adolescence.

Uncertainty is caused by the consciousness of not knowing what to do and what is the matter. We feel uncertain when we have to face a still unknown or an altogether new situation. The uncertainty of youth is doubled by the fact that not only the objective world but also the subjective are unknown and bewildering.

When confronted by the unknown, the typical reaction of a mind, especially of one not sure of itself, is anguish or anxiety. The close relation between anxiety and the unknown has been pointed out repeatedly by modern psychology, which indeed has paid greater attention to these things than the psychology of old. Everybody who has to face a quite new and unwonted situation becomes the victim of anxiety, unless some other factor prevails sufficiently to counterbalance this feeling.

Children always become the easy prey of anxiety, since they find themselves in a strange and unknown world. If they are not anxious habitually, but only in exceptional situations, it is because they feel protected by the adults surrounding them. The very moment they become frightened or anxious, they turn for help and shelter to the mother.

The presence of anxiety is often overlooked by an observer, and even by the subject himself. Anxiety, like many other mental states, may mask itself beneath types of behavior which eventually seem just the opposite of fearfulness. He who whistles while walking through a dark wood, is afraid notwithstanding his external display of courage; but this very display may convince him and others of his courage.

The uncertainty of adolescence cannot but create a tendency towards anxiety. But feeling afraid, especially if there is no tangible reason, makes a man ashamed. He will then attempt to hide his fear from others and from himself. This is just the way of adolescents. They feel urged to behave in this manner all the more because they look forward to becoming within a short time adults themselves, and, because of the habits developed during childhood, they still regard the adults as essentially unafraid. It is, accordingly, often difficult to discover the signs of anxiety in an adolescent. The well-known process of compensation and over-compensation tends to veil the manifestations of anxiety and of uncertainty. Desiring to convince themselves of their courage, of their self-assurance, of their capacity to face reality, the adolescents overdo very often the behavior intended for this end. A good deal of what impresses the casual observer as rudeness, rashness, exaggerated self-assertion, is due in adolescents to an attempt to hide their basic uncertainty.

If one wants to make sure of the existence of anxiety, be it in children or in adolescents, one has to study very carefully their total behavior. They may be courageous, even foolhardy, and nevertheless show in certain situations definite signs of fear or anxiety. To know a person one has to become acquainted with his behavior in all the many sides of his relation to reality. One indeed knows nothing at all of a boy when he is observed only in the classroom. How he behaves on the playground, how at home, how when with friends, how when left to himself, how when working and how when idling, etc. — all this has to be known before we can form a somewhat reliable opinion on his personality.

Observation is the more necessary, since the adolescent is difficult of approach. He does not want any one to guess at his true state of mind. He does not even want to become quite conscious of this state himself. He is reticent and resents very much being questioned, though he may, on the other hand and occasionally, be very glad of an opportunity to talk of himself, and even more so to be told (without having to say very much himself) what the matter is with him. This attitude is not exclusively one of adolescence. There are adults too who may want another to know certain things, but who recoil from telling them. This is possibly due to a certain persistence of traits which really belong to adolescence; this kind of behavior is not uncommon with people afflicted with neurotic troubles, and it has been said not unjustly that neurosis implies something of "juvenilism," of a persistence of behavior features characteristic of adolescence.

Adolescents are, as is well known, rather inclined to criticize everything. Whatever the older generation holds to be right is ridiculous to the adolescent. He feels that laws and rules ought to be changed. He is easily captivated by all kinds of new and revolutionary ideas. Being keenly conscious of his newly awakened personality and its uniqueness, he easily develops a kind of relativism, making "man the measure of all things." Objective and eternal truths are doubted; the very existence of such truths becomes questionable to the adolescent mind. If one refers him to such truths or to laws which have proved valid throughout the centuries, he is not impressed at all; for him the world is as new and as ambiguous as he feels his own personality to be. When the adolescent's reason becomes aware of its individuality, it is no longer willing to accept statements that were believed but a short time ago and are still upheld as the very laws of existence by his elders. The ever-changing aspect of the world, corresponding to the continuous changes going on within his own personality, makes values appear uncertain and vague, since what was attractive yesterday may become repulsive to-morrow, and since for the unsophisticated mind attraction and repulsion are the very characteristics by which to recognize values and non-values.

Changing though their ideas may be, young people are nevertheless deadly in earnest about them. They regard their ideas and feelings as much more important than those which older people speak of; this is partly the result of the impression that all these things are absolutely new and have never been thought of or felt before. This tendency to consider one's own experiences as quite singular is not limited to the adolescent's mind. It is well to be aware of the features which adolescent mentality has in common with not unfrequent types of adult mentality, because this may help us somehow in understanding the former. Many people, then, feel definitely shocked at being told that their feelings, and maybe their symptoms, are well known. It is quite common to hear someone say, after he has reported on some mental difficulty: "Have you ever heard such a thing?" He is very astonished when he is told that one has. This idea of uniqueness, whether of the adolescent or of an adult, is indeed true in one way, since every individual is indeed quite unique and since his personal experience has an absolutely unique note; but the idea is wrong in the sense in which it is understood by most of those who hold it. The uniqueness is conditioned by some indefinable quality and by the fact of this experience belonging to this one individual and to no other one; but there is, generally, no uniqueness of contents. It is the how of experience which is the basis of uniqueness, but not the what of experience. The more, however, an individual is impressed by the peculiar quality of his personal experience, the more he is inclined to believe that the whole of it, even the factual content, is altogether new. This impression of novelty is exceedingly strong in adolescents; they take, therefore, all remarks pointing to the frequency of similar experiences as a sure sign of a lack of understanding.

If you want to know an adolescent, you have to gain his confidence. If you want to gain his confidence, you have, first of all, to take his ideas and problems seriously.

Discarding his ideas as unripe, making light of his difficulties, telling him that these things come to everyone and will pass away (as has happened with all those who have become old enough to see the futility of these problems and difficulties), refusing to listen to him because it has been thus with boys and girls since time immemorial—all these well-known attitudes of adults, born partly from their being disenchanted, partly from envy, partly simply from laziness and evasion of responsibilities, are the surest way of estranging the young person and of creating a profound cleavage which will never again be closed.

It is, of course, quite right to tell the adolescent that his troubles are not unique in the sense he believes them to be; but this has to be said tactfully and with caution. Only after having got the youngster to feel that one understands him and is willing to listen and to advise, may one point out to him that all these troubles belong to human nature, that they have indeed a peculiar note, first with adolescents in general, secondly with him as an individual; that even adult life is not altogether free of them. But it would be a mistake to cut short his tale by stating that one has heard these very things already many times.

The natural thing for the adolescent to do in his fits of perplexity is to turn to his parents. Some do, because they have parents who make this possible. But in a great many cases the relation between parents and child has become so badly strained that this turning to father and mother is out of the question. Not because the parents do not love the child, and not because the child has lost all feelings of affection for the parents, but because the latter do not know how to deal with him, and because they have indeed long years before barred their way to his mind. Scores of little things which passed unnoticed and which were believed to be of no importance have accumulated to form a barrier secluding the well-meaning parents from the confidence of their child. Character education of adolescents should begin in early childhood; the way to influence must be kept open and not become barred by misunderstandings and the many little shocks which finally shatter the original confidence of the child.

Because of this previous history it is often definitely more difficult for parents than for an outsider — nay, it is often quite impossible for the parents — to establish closer contact with the mind of the adolescent. The parents, in such a case, have as great a need to seek for a way of approach as has the outsider. The latter is indeed often more fortunate, because he is not associated with many half-forgotten but nonetheless influential memories. Sad though it may be for the parents, it is quite true that strangers are not seldom much more successful with adolescents than parents or even other people who have known the youngsters for many years.

A stranger or outsider has, it is true, to discover some way of approach. If the adolescent resents the prying of the parents into his affairs, he at least admits, if grudgingly, that they have some right, or at least that they may believe they have it. But the stranger has no right at all, unless it be given to him by the adolescent himself. Unasked-for advice is never welcome—with the adolescent even less than with any other person.

There may be, indeed, some cases or situations in which an understanding person, one who is gifted with the necessary psychological insight and the necessary tact, may venture to offer his advice or at least to explain his ideas to an adolescent without being asked to do so. Sometimes we may see a young mind evidently in trouble, needing help, perhaps desiring it, but too shy or too self-conscious to ask for it. In such a case one might risk offering help; but this too has to be done with a certain caution if one is to avoid scaring away the adolescent.

In the majority of cases, however, it is necessary to prepare slowly and pertinaciously a way of approach. This takes time; but the time is not lost. While we still are far from enjoying the youngster's confidence, we may come to know him better, and he may, without being really aware of it, come to trust us and to show a certain disposition to get in closer touch with us.

Since a premature attempt to touch on the actual problems may result in failure, it will be best for us to try an approach from some more peripherical point. We must look for something we may have in common with the boy or the girl. The adolescent mind generally regards the older generation as so utterly different that any attempt to make them see is hopeless. "They," as many a boy or girl terms the older people, do not understand, and one cannot make them see. There is nothing in common between old and young—such a conviction is very prevalent among youth. Young people, therefore, often prefer to turn to others of their own age. It is, of course, quite true that "youth belongs to youth," as the saying goes. Only young people can be playmates of the young, and only they will indeed understand many of the interests and problems the adolescent mind harbors. This sympathy and understanding on the part of people of the same age may be very comforting in one sense; it is disappointing in another. This understanding is based more on the subjective note of personal experience, than on any comprehension of the real content or the real meaning of the problems. The exclusive communion of young people with one another may increase their confusion and uncertainty instead of lessening them. It may be that two confused minds will help each other to a better understanding, if their confusion is not about the very same points. But if both of them have equally confused ideas on the very same problem, it is simply impossible for them to help each other to see more clearly.

Even if the danger of bad example, mutual encouragement in some rather unreasonable attitudes, and suchlike things be disregarded for the moment, the fact just alluded to must be considered. Of course, it would be quite wrong and, for that matter, useless to hinder young people from meeting and being together. But it is equally wrong to believe that, if thrown together and left to themselves, they will profit more and get over their difficulties more easily than if they remain in touch also with older people.

Approaching them from some neutral and, as has been said before, more peripherical point has many advantages. By attempting a too personal and too abrupt an approach we are almost sure to awaken their opposition. They will look askance at us, and either (when they are rather rude) question our right to be interested in them at all or even tell us to mind our own business, or (if they have a little manners) assume an arrogant and unapproachable pose. Arrogance and conceit are due, to a great extent, to the fact that the adolescents have lost courage and self-reliance. They attribute the uncertainty which has got hold of them (and of which, try as they may, they cannot but be conscious) to some defects of their personality; they feel that they ought to be sure of themselves, sure of knowing their way in reality, sure of the answers to the many questions which worry them. But they will not admit this, either to themselves or to others; they will rather try to silence the troubling voices of their interior by acting as if they were quite sure of themselves and of everything in this world.

Unless we find the adolescent in a situation which, so to say, forces his hand, or unless we are in the eyes of the adolescent endowed with a special authority (which is generally more due to personality, perhaps to repute, than to any official or semiofficial position), we ought to beware of a direct attack. A roundabout way and a gradual approach are much more advisable. The nearer, of course, the point we chose for establishing contact with the adolescent is to his personal problems, the better. Being on good terms with young people on the playground, for instance, is no guarantee of a successful approach in personal matters. There may be indeed some occasions which permit such an approach: certain mistakes of behavior, unfairness in play, unwillingness to accept defeat, or a certain lack of magnanimity towards a beaten competitor may become points for useful discussion. But even such a discussion will be possible only after some kind of personal relationship has become established.

Many believe that sport and a common interest in it offer a special opportunity for approaching adolescents. But this view may be altogether mistaken. Interests may be very strong, and nevertheless be too peripherical, in so far as their objects are not of a kind to reach down to the depth of personality. The enormous rôle played by sport to-day, especially in the minds of young people, is a quite characteristic feature of our times. It is wrong to compare this interest in sport with the "same" attitude as it existed a century or more ago in England and in America. The "same" attitude acquires a different signification according to the general background. An age which afforded but few opportunities for amusement or relaxation necessarily differed greatly in its attitude towards sport from an era which by radio and pictures, by the wide distribution of the printed word, by the possibilities of many kinds of intellectual enjoyment, is capable of satisfying in countless ways the longing for diversity, for stimulation, for things other than the toil of the working day.

It is not for these pages to indulge in a discussion of the psychology of sport, or rather of the great interest it has for a very large majority. But we must refer to the fact that this interest in sport in young people is due, among other reasons, to their desire to escape from the disquieting problems which they are doing their utmost to ignore. Sports, either participated in or witnessed, offer a rare chance for this escape. The excitement caused by games, in which there are after all winners and losers, is one reason why this kind of enjoyment is so effective in the sense we just mentioned. Another reason is that the adolescents feel that, when they are interested and even wrapped up in sport, they are but doing what their elders also do; here for once they find something they may enjoy, and which is not disapproved by the elder generation. Let us point out, incidentally, that all the good effects of games which are put forward by the enthusiastic admirers of these activities, exist exclusively for those who are themselves active participants, but not at all for those who enjoy games merely as spectators. Sport may have quite a good influence on the general development of character—how far this is true, remains to be determined; but witnessing games has probably no influence at all, if indeed it has not a rather undesirable one.

It is true that every aspect and every interest of a person reveals something of his inner structure and general character. But there are some aspects which reveal more, and others which are, so to say, so far from the core of personality that they possess little significance. But to understand a personality fully, one has to penetrate into the very depth of his inner being. A general knowledge of the characteristic features of a person's age, sex, class, etc., is quite insufficient. It is not even enough to be acquainted in a general way with the person's ways of life. The separate observations we may collect by studying his behavior in various conditions and situations must be synthesized into a complete and self-consistent picture of this individual. It needs a quite unusual sharpsightedness—a quality which the average person cannot claim to possess—to detect the nature of an individual by casual observations. As a rule, we have to make a complete study of him, even if his behavior appears to be so "typical" as to need no further investigation. Typical though an individual may appear to be, he is nevertheless a representative of his type in his own and individual manner.

Personality, being a "whole," will reveal something of its nature in any phase of behavior whatsoever. There is, therefore, no phase of behavior which might be justly called uninteresting. Every observation is worthy of note. We have to be glad whenever an adolescent is willing to talk to us of things which interest him, even when these things seem to be rather far from what we really want to ascertain. The fact, however, of his being interested in such and such things is in itself quite characteristic. Sometimes we may be able to inquire into the reasons of this interest, and thereby discover a little more of this youth's inner personality. It is a mistake to dismiss such confidences and to say: "Well, all right, but I want to hear of your real difficulties."

To-day, however, the interests of youth are unfortunately of a kind which does not promise much in the line of discovery of personality. In an age in which intellectual and cultural problems were held in higher esteem, approach was somewhat easier; discussions on general problems or on questions bordering on philosophy led rather soon to a revelation of personal attitudes. The more the average interest turns on values of a lesser order, the more difficult it becomes to gain access to the personal problems. There are two reasons for this. The one is, of course,

that the real problems of man are related to the higher
and highest values; the real problems even of the common, the non-intellectual, man may be rightly termed me-
taphysical; they are concerned with the place of the individual man within the totality of being, with individual
rights and duties, with the nature of man, with the soul,
with God. They are mostly concerned with God, strange
though this statement may seem; but one has only to look
at the passion displayed by those who stand for "free
thought," for atheism, for "enlightenment," to discover
that the true problem is God, His existence, His commandments. Otherwise, the impassioned criticisms, the de-
nouncements of believers as reactionary, as deplorable derelicts of "dark ages," etc., would be altogether incomprehensible. The second reason why lower interests are of little
avail for the revelation of personality is that these interests
are frequently the common property of nearly all adolescents; they therefore become in a way standardized, they
lose all personal note, and the result is a certain lack of
differentiation. They are, so to say, conventional; the enthusiasm they arouse is no argument against their being
fashioned according to one, rather conventional, pattern.
This pattern develops the more easily, since a value allows
for so much less variations of attitude, the lower it ranks
in the scale of values. Mere sensual pleasure, for instance,
as caused by food or drink, may be appreciated or not, but
there is hardly a possibility of sharply differentiated attitudes. One likes games and is interested in them, or one
dislikes them and is indifferent to them; here again there
is hardly a chance of a wide variety of attitudes developing.

But even superficial interests may lead to a closer acquaintance with personalities. First, let it be noted that superficiality of interest and enthusiasm are not mutually exclusive; depth of interest depends not so much on the subjective attitude as on the nature of the object, whereas enthusiasm is, of course, a merely subjective reaction. The common phrase of being "deeply interested" is rather unfortunate; it would be better to say "strongly interested." There are certain values which never can enter into the depth of personality, because there is a close interrelation between the kind of a value and the "layers" of personality touched by the value. We cannot, however, indulge in a more detailed discussion of this point, though it is probably of tremendous importance for a theory of education and its practice, too.

The interest young people develop in moving pictures is generally equally superficial. They are often—and it is not different with many adults—more interested in definite actor-personalities than in the plot or in the picture as such. This interest in personalities is generally dictated by convention or by "publicity"; there is rarely anything original and "personal" in it. By discussing, however, a play and the reasons why it is liked or why pictures are gifted with such an enthralling power, one may sometimes become aware of deeper and carefully hidden attitudes. If we are able to find out why a certain character in a picture is liked and why another is felt to be repulsive, why one story is adjudged interesting and another as dull, we might indeed get a glimpse into the adolescent's personality. A discussion on the theatre or on reading is often more fruitful. But here again we encounter the obstacle of standardization and superficiality. The stuff which most of the young people read does not indeed lend itself to an analysis of deeper attitudes. Magazine stories, which apparently supply nearly all their reading material, are rather uniform. There are, of course, several types; but within the general frame of each of these types there is but little variety and even less originality. In some of these magazines one may come across, indeed, quite good stories of a truly artistic value and noteworthy for the sentiments expressed therein; but this is a rare occurrence. Moreover, the magazines which publish such stories are not the ones the average adolescent prefers. His predilection is for another type, and he apparently abhors especially a longer story. A discussion of the average type of reading, of "Wild-West tales," of criminal novels and "mysteries," etc., will probably not prove very useful, though one never really knows. And, as has been remarked before, it would be definitely unwise to neglect any opening whatever.

Sometimes, even when discussing very superficial things with an adolescent, one may become suddenly aware of some fundamental trait of personality. It would not be advisable to jump, so to say, at this discovery. It is better to let it pass unnoticed, without comment though not unremarked. By collecting such evidences one is enabled to make, at a later time, a true estimate of how the young mind feels, and by this to make the adolescent realize that we are, after all, capable of understanding him. He gets this impression particularly when we are capable of predicting some attitude of his. We may, for instance, have discovered a definite trend towards sentimentality in a boy who generally acts as if feelings and emotions, especially of a more tender kind, were quite foreign to his personality. He may one day mention having seen a picture, or having read a story of a rather sentimental character; a casual remark, "I suppose you liked the thing," may throw him off his guard and make him ask, rather astonished: "How did you guess?"

It rarely does good, however, to attempt to get hold of the adolescent's mind by surprise. Unless he is already willing to confide in us and needs but a little help to pass over the last obstacles, he does not want to be found out, though he may be very desirous of telling us what is in his mind. But surprise may prove to be a shock and scare him away. It is better for us to proceed slowly and with much patience.

There are, of course, cases in which patience and caution are out of place. When we see a youngster becoming involved in some dangerous error, we cannot avoid tackling him directly. But even then we ought to think before acting. The outcome is always rather doubtful. The intervention of authority may provoke an even stronger attitude of revolt, and impel the adolescent in the very direction which we so much want him to shun.

The approach becomes more difficult still because of the oscillations of the adolescent mind, its swinging from an excessive interest in the inner life to an equally exclusive and exaggerated interest in external things, and changing with an often surprising swiftness from one interest to another. Consequently, a way of approach which seemed to present itself to-day may be impassable to-morrow. The change of interests in things is conditioned partly by the adolescent's shunning of effort and difficulties. This is due not only to the natural laziness of man—which is perhaps a little overrated in common opinion—but also to the adolescent's distrust of his own capacities. He dreads failure because failure would prove to him that his distrust in himself is justified; the conflict between his growing sense of being an individuality, a person in his own right, and his feeling still totally at a loss, would become intensified by such an experience, which he accordingly, by instinct as it were, avoids.

Much may be gained by interesting young people in some topic higher than just baseball, Wild-West tales, or shallow amusements. We shall return to this point in a later chapter.

When we are dealing with young people (or, for that matter, with older too), no quality is of greater importance than patience. If we wish to be of help, we must wait until an opportunity is offered to us. The better we know how to wait, the more surely will such an opportunity be given to us. In the meantime we can do nothing but try to keep on as good terms with the youngsters as possible, and to amass whatever information we may get. Everything is worthy of consideration, whether it is of personal observation or is reported by third persons. But we must keep those things in our minds and not hurl them at the boy or girl, even if we feel definitely shocked by what we have been told. The too often used challenge, "What is this that I hear of you?" ought to be discarded altogether. Young people do not want to be spied upon, they do not like feeling controlled, and they are easily scared away, because they are so very anxious to preserve what they call their independence.

There is, of course, one exception to be made. Here, as everywhere else, the *bonum commune* takes precedence of every *bonum privatum*. If we become aware that the behavior of some youngster is endangering the morality or, generally speaking, the personality of another, or of several others, we cannot but intervene.

But we must beware of hasty judgments. We must always bear in mind that many of the undesirable traits which young people show are but rudimentary forms of features which will be unobjectionable in the adult personality. The adult has to be independent in his decisions; he has to take the whole responsibility for his actions; and, though he may listen to the advice of others, he has to make up his mind all by himself. The habit of depending on the advice of others is an easy way of getting rid of responsibility. Young people are not as yet able to decide for themselves, but they have to learn how to do it. It is dangerous to influence them too much; a short time later they will have to build up their own lives, and they will be fully responsible for their actions.

Adolescence is a period of preparation and of training. Training means acquiring a faculty not yet developed. We ought not to be shocked by the clumsiness of the youthful attempts to master reality. No teacher will reprove a pupil for not being capable of doing what he is just beginning to learn. Rebuking youth sternly is not the right way of approach.

It is generally believed that adolescents are difficult to understand. In a way this is true, but only as long as we either look at youth from the point of view of the adult or think of the adolescent as being still a child. If one has become fully aware of the general mentality of youth and has taken the trouble to find out enough about this one individual's particular situation, the difficulty generally disappears. One can then understand and even predict his behavior. But to be capable of such an understanding, one has to become intimately acquainted with all the separate features of his personality and his life.

The latter term includes not only personal behavior, but also environmental conditions. It is often very difficult or even impossible to understand a person if one does not know what kind of influence he is subjected to, when we are not observing him. His previous history is, moreover, equally important. Many of his reactions are not mere answers to the actual situation, but are largely moulded by his previous experiences.

There is nothing, either in an individual's present state or in his history, that is uninteresting, and nothing that we might justly call negligible. To find a way of approach we have, first of all, to keep our eyes open, to rid ourselves of all prejudices, and to observe with the cool mind of the scientist.

One great difficulty has to be mentioned. The adolescent desires, in the depths of his soul, to become the object of personal interest to someone he likes; but he resents, at the same time, all display of sentiment and, more than anything, of pity. There are but very few moments when he will be grateful for being pitied. One has, accordingly, to find a middle way; one has to make the youngster guess at one's personal interest, so that he will not feel being but the object of a perfunctory attitude or merely of a psychological study. One must, however, beware of displaying too much of this interest. Keeping just the mean between these attitudes is the more important since we have to avoid strengthening the "introverted" attitude and the withdrawal from reality. But this may easily occur if, by an undue interest in his inner life, we turn the adolescent still more towards introspection and self-analysis.

Chapter III

Ways of Influencing the Adolescent

GIVEN THE PECULIARITIES of the mental make-up of adolescents and the difficulties of approaching them, the problem of how to influence and to guide youth becomes indeed a very perplexing one. All influencing and all guidance rest on a clear understanding of the individual case, and on the possibility of establishing contact with the deeper "layers" of personality. Another condition underlying a successful guidance is evidently a certain constancy in the personality which one aspires to guide. None of these conditions seem to be realized in the case of adolescents. We do not know them sufficiently, at least not under ordinary conditions; we cannot establish such close contact as to gain a real influence over them; we cannot rely on their being the same to-day as they were yesterday, and we cannot, accordingly, know whether a method of guidance which at one time seemed adequate will prove successful even a short time afterwards.

But there are still other obstacles which make the task of guidance a particularly arduous one. The adolescent inclines, as has been already explained, towards a relativistic view of truths and values. He is no longer disposed to take any order of values for granted, simply because it is that which his parents or some other persons of authority believe to be the right one. He will accept only laws and statements of which he himself approves. But his "self" is not yet sufficiently consolidated to afford any stability of views; it has just grown out of childhood. The adolescent, therefore, feels that the old rules and laws which had been accepted on authority or in a naïve manner need revision. If he is intelligent enough to see a point of view not his own, he will concede that the opinion of others may be right, but he feels at the same time that he has first to make sure of this, before he can accept their opinion. In the meantime, things are in suspense. The adolescent can no longer subscribe to the old ideas, nor can he definitely replace them by others. His mind is in a state of doubt and tossed from one extreme attitude into another. The inevitable result is that the adolescent assumes mainly an attitude of denial. Young people are quick in rejecting views held by the older generation, but they are not capable of replacing these ideas with others.

This fact explains a feature of the adolescent mind which is very often deplored or criticized, but seldom really understood. Young people are attracted, in a marked way, by all kinds of revolutionary and destructive ideas. Dissatisfaction with the existing state of things always leads to the adoption of disruptive views, but these are not always succeeded by constructive ideas. The longing to see things changed creates at first a merely destructive tendency. To develop constructive plans demands a more complete understanding of the actual situation than the average mind usually possesses. The adolescent mind indeed knows nothing, or scarcely anything, of such constructive ideas, and cannot possibly know of them, because it does not yet possess a sufficient knowledge of reality. The dissatisfaction, born partly out of the contrast between the adolescent's personality and his surroundings and partly out of his being conscious of his own incompleteness and uncertainty, gives rise to an intense desire for change; the adolescent is fretting under the pressure of the antagonism which is the necessary and natural result of his internal and external situation. Since the adolescent feels that he cannot subscribe to any traditional idea, he is impelled towards all that contradicts such ideas, simply because it contradicts, and not because of the intrinsic value of the new views. He is attracted by the revolutionary side of a thing, independently of its material content. And because this formal factor of external antagonism has become decisive, the adolescent furthermore is very much inclined to change his ideas, to adopt this kind of antagonistic view to-day and another one to-morrow. Incidentally, this is the reason why all kinds of radicalism find so many supporters among young people—irrespective of the particular ideas, if only they are radical. This is the reason, too, why the adolescent is capable of adopting objectively contradictory ideas without any apparent difficulty; he does not really care for their material side, though he may, as long as his enthusiasm survives, defend them with all the energy of apparent conviction; he cares only for the formal side of being revolutionary, radical, and so forth.

Traditional views are upheld by authority, and authority is the only reason why the child believes, according to his lights, in these views. The child is not yet capable of understanding and of justifying these ideas rationally; he relies on authority. Authority, however, is one of the things that adolescents most resent. It is, strange enough, at the same time one of the things for which they long most.

This ambiguous situation is easily explained by the ambiguity of the total situation characteristic of the adolescent mind. The denial of authority springs from the growing consciousness which the adolescent feels of being a person in his own right; the desire for authority springs from his uncertainty which seeks relief. The first factor makes it impossible for him to accept a statement merely on authority, because this would be tantamount to abdicating his right of independent decision; the uncertainty makes it impossible for him to decide definitely on some view, because he possesses a sufficient knowledge neither of reality nor of his own ego. The result of these conflicting influences either is an often rapid switching from one set of ideas to another (although possibly the second set absolutely contradicts the first), or it is a kind of compromise in which certain types of authority are rejected altogether, while others are accepted gladly and with an amazing lack of criticism. Because of this peculiar structure of the adolescent mind we see quite frequently the very same youngsters who revolt against some traditional authority (of parents, of teachers, or of the Church) astonishingly ready to submit to some other authority. This other authority is sometimes that of a revolutionary party, and sometimes that of an individual person who for some reason exercises a peculiar influence and is admired, loved, and blindly obeyed in a way which seems quite incompatible with the adolescent's general attitude of revolt. One reason for this is the adolescent's craving for an authority to rely upon; this, however, has to be other than the old one which (sometimes not without its own fault) has lost its prestige, and against which all the revolutionary forces, all the strivings for independence, all the will for self-assertion are directed. Another reason, of a more positive nature, is that the new authority appears as the representative and the visible embodiment of the new order.

Education has to take account of this state of things. It might even use, for its own ends, the adolescent's desire for authority, if it knew the right way to handle the situation. Authority as such does not impress youthful minds. Simply to assert authority is rather a way to make the young people more restive and more disinclined to listen or to obey. The adolescent is no longer like the child who either trusted implicitly, and therefore obeyed even if he at first remonstrated, or who felt that the adults know better in any case. But it may be quite useful to point out, even to a child, that he has to do what he is told, not simply because it is father and mother who say so, but because they are bound to know better. The adolescent is impressed only when authority either defends ideas akin to his own (and since his ideas are apt to change rather quickly, the authority of to-day may become unimpressive to-morrow), or when he can be made to see the rights and the necessity on which such authority is predicated.

In so far, therefore, as authority is concerned, the task of education in adolescence is much less the maintaining of this authority than building it up. This problem has become probably more difficult in modern times than it has been ever before. The general mentality of an historical period and the particular political and economical situation are not without a definite influence in such matters. It has been always thus, and it is even more so to-day. The general situation has a more direct bearing on every person's life and existence than ever in the past. Each man's personality becomes colored, as it were, by the factors determining the general situation. Even if one is willing to ignore politics, even if one is in a relatively secure economic position, one cannot help feeling somehow the general uncertainty pervading the modern world. In periods of general uncertainty, of increasing economic or political difficulties, of conflicting social and philosophical views, youth feels its own uncertainty more keenly than ever. It is perhaps because of this factor that one sees the young people in some countries so amazingly ready to join military organizations, to submit to very stern rules, and to obey the authorities ruling over these organizations. If they join by their own free will, they are submitting to an authority they have chosen themselves, and not to one which is imposed on them. If they have to join because of a law establishing such a duty, they do so because they are told that this whole matter belongs already to the future, that it is the beginning of a realization of that future of which they themselves are the representatives. To become a member of such an organization, moreover, gives the adolescent the consciousness of belonging somewhere, of doing things he is capable of doing and entitled to do; it gives him a certain feeling of importance which he cannot develop as long as he stands more or less isolatedly against the closed front of the adult world.

Sometimes boys or girls of a good and well-to-do family will join a revolutionary organization—become members of the Communist party, for instance. They claim they do this out of idealism, because they feel so strongly the injustice done to the working classes, because they are enthusiastic about general justice, a better distribution of wealth, and a general reconstruction of society. Idealism and similar longings, which may be quite praiseworthy, though misdirected, play here a certain rôle, no doubt. But the very same aims could be pursued also in a different manner—for instance, by taking the Commandments of God and the Church more seriously. Why, then, join just the Communists? The psychology of adolescence, as it has been sketched in these pages, gives an answer. The reaction against authority depends very much on the intensity with which the outward uncertainty imposes itself, or on the relative strength of the outer and the inner elements composing the mental situation of the adolescent. Once again a warning may be uttered against premature generalizations. The reasons why an individual adolescent revolts at all, and why he chooses one particular way of expressing his revolutionary attitude, have to be found out by a careful individual analysis.

Authority which is inefficient is worse than no authority at all. Authority is of some avail only when it can make itself accepted by the adolescent. The authority of personalities is, therefore, generally greater than the authority of institutions. The adolescent succumbs easily to the fascination of a personality, whereas an impersonal institution may leave him cold. His mind being thrown into the turmoil of uncertainty, he has a desire for some visible, concrete, impressive power on which to rely; an institution, even if it is in a way admired and acknowledged, has not this capacity of immediately impressing the youthful mind. The respect for and the acknowledgment of institutions depend, therefore, very much on the persons representing them and presenting them to adolescents. The mere fact that a person is objectively vested with some authority is not sufficient to guarantee an impression on the adolescent mind.

This point is the more necessary to emphasize since we cannot well leave it to the individual to discover or rediscover the sense and the necessity of authority. If we do so, we may easily let the individual become entangled in mistakes which may prove impossible to correct in later years, even though the individual's initial error may meanwhile have been exposed. Man is too much inclined to find fault with others and with circumstances, and too little willing to acknowledge the mistakes he himself has committed. We may indeed trust in human nature, and hope that when an error is disclosed, either by facts or by reasoning, it will be corrected. But it is doubtful whether an individual will become aware at all of the error; if he is told that he committed it, he will accuse his critic of not understanding the matter or of being hostile, envious, or what not, rather than acknowledge the mistake. To convince a man of his error usually takes more time than even the best-intentioned adviser has at his disposal; and it is practically impossible that every one should find another willing to convince him of his error. And even if this were the case, it would not be enough: a man must not only be shown that he has made mistakes and where; he must be taught how to correct them and how to deal with all the consequences to which these errors may already have led. But to repair all the consequences of a mistake is often impossible; a man is quite frequently caught so completely in the meshes of his errors that he is incapable of extricating himself.

"A little error made in the beginning may have fearful effects at the end," says St. Thomas, quoting the Greek philosopher, Aristotle. It is the same with philosophy as with every other thing—with individual life and society, with moral development and efficiency, with true faith and with human relations. To ensure a desirable development of the adolescent, one has to prepare the way during childhood; to enable a man to find his way to truth and to the right manner of living, one has to take preparatory measures while he still is young. Many have had to discover in later years, often at a high cost, the necessity and the advantage of authority. Many have got into trouble because of their not realizing in time the claim of authority to our allegiance. Establishing the right relation to authority is, therefore, one of the main tasks of education during adolescence.

A brutal and "authoritative" assertion of authority will be of no avail; it will, in fact, probably have just the opposite effect to that intended. We must discover other ways for making authority acceptable to the adolescents. There are, in the main, but two ways. Authority may become established on the basis of personal relations, or it may become acceptable because its necessity and its true meaning are approved by reason. The second way, if practicable, is definitely superior. Reasons, once they are really understood and have become, as it were, part of the personality, are independent of time; what is true remains so whatever changes may take place in our circumstances. Personal relations, however, are subject to all kinds of influences; emotional factors, accidental circumstances, and the almost inevitable disturbances of such relations may destroy even those which seemed to be most firmly established.

The greatest threat to authority based on personal relations lies in the person of him who is invested with authority. Even children will not accept authority without a certain amount of questioning. Even to them authority has to justify its demands and to live up, as it were, to them. Authority runs the danger of destroying itself as soon as it becomes extravagant in its demands and exaggerates its rights. Nothing is more capable of destroying authority than the pretense of infallibility. No man is infallible; no one is sure of being always right. It may happen that in a particular case the child is right and the parents are wrong. It would then be a grave mistake for the latter not to realize and not to avow this. The discovery that even his parents may be wrong is sometimes a shock to the child who still believes them to be omniscient and almighty. But the shock is much greater if the child discovers that his parents are not only liable to error, but also capable of insincerity. As a matter of fact, an open avowal of an error does not diminish authority; it even strengthens the bond between child and parents, because their relation thus becomes, so to say, more human. Although the belief in the parents' infallibility disappears, something more valuable is gained. The intellectual authority, if one may express it in this way, becomes less, but the moral authority grows.

Authority can never expect to see demands fulfilled which itself ignores. The criticism of adolescents—and for that matter of children too—is directed not so much against authority as such, as against authority which believes itself exempted from its own rules. The *quod-licet-Jovi* idea has to be handled with great caution. There are, of course, many things permitted to adults which cannot be conceded to the child or to the adolescent; but the youngsters must know that these things will be accessible to them too after a certain time, and, in so far as possible, must be told why the adults may do or have this or that, while the younger generation is still denied the permission. Though they may be unable to think these things out quite clearly, children as well as adolescents distinguish very well between rules which apply to adults as such and others which are conditioned by development. It is true that this capacity of discernment becomes somewhat blunted in adolescents, because the longing to be already grown up, to be really what the young mind feels itself to be, though for the present but potentially, tends to lessen the sharpness of distinction. But even the adolescent may be made to see these differences, especially if the older people take care to explain to him how things stand, and why he ought still to abstain from this or from that.

Authority, however, which disregards rules that are

evidently of a general nature and are felt to be binding either for everyone or for nobody, very soon loses all its influence. It is in this sense that authority has to be above all criticism. We must not resent the critical attitude of the younger generation, but should be very careful not to supply real reasons for it. Authority which asserts itself unduly and enforces its demands will often not be aware at all of the critical attitude of the "subjects." The latter will refrain from uttering their criticisms and disapproval, because they feel that they will be misunderstood in any case, and that, therefore, it is both useless and inexpedient to say what is in their minds. But this secret revolt and this hidden criticism threaten authority more surely than an open outbreak, because they undermine gradually all belief in authority—in that of this particular person first, and by an easy generalization in all authority whatsoever.

The problem of authority is so very critical because we have to steer a middle course between two equally bad extremes—a course which is indeed often quite difficult to hold. We must neither exaggerate authority so as to make it utterly disgusting to the adolescent, nor may we dispense with it and thereby fail to develop a true sense for authority and order.

There is a certain school of pedagogues who believe ardently in the expediency of abolishing the distance between the pedagogue and the adolescent. They want the pedagogue to be the friend, even the comrade, of the adolescent. There is some truth underlying this idea, but there is a rather great degree of error, too. It is true that by treating young people almost as equals one establishes contact with them more easily; they may feel more at home and not be afraid of being "preached to," which is a thing they dread very much. Thus, this abolition of all distance becomes a way of establishing authority, but one has to display quite an amount of tact—and of tactics. This mode of establishing authority is successful only when the distance is not really abolished; the equalization of pedagogue and pupil must not go so far that they both become persons of absolutely equal rights. If this were the case, all influence could be gained only when and in so far as the pupil is willingly acquiescent. The distance should be abolished only in so far as to avoid wounding the susceptibilities of the adolescents. One must indeed abstain from treating them as if they were mere children and altogether incapable of seeing things. Even children generally have a much greater capacity of understanding than they are commonly credited with. In placing himself on exactly the same level with the adolescent, however, the pedagogue renounces every possibility of creating a real understanding of authority; and without such an understanding the further development of the adolescent, especially in his attitude towards work and towards social life, will probably go amiss.

When the older generation wishes to enforce its authority, it very often refers to its experiences. This, however, is an argument which generally leaves the adolescent quite cold; he is not impressed at all by experience undergone by older people. In this feeling he is, indeed, not altogether wrong. Experience does not represent something uniform and something objective; its value depends very much on the person who has undergone the experience. Most of the facts we come across in our lives are subject to very different interpretations; what interpretation one gives to them depends on what kind of person one is. If the peculiar point of view from which a man regards reality is not shared by his hearer, the latter will neither profit by the experience of the first nor even feel it to be worth considering. The adolescent has a very strong impression of belonging to a different age from his parents'; the experiences they refer to occurred so many years ago. He is aware of the difference in the times, of problems being no longer the same, of ideas having changed; and he feels, accordingly, that the opposition of the older generation is due to a lack of understanding, to a clinging to obsolete and mistaken views, to their incapacity to grasp the signs of the new era.

It is natural for everyone to associate with his equals. No wonder, then, that the adolescent seeks the company of others of his age. He is, however, very much disposed to take their ideas as representing absolute truth. His discovery of others who share more or less the same attitude strengthens his antagonism as well as his power of resistance. He feels at home with his comrades not only because of the features common to him and to them as being of the same age, but also because they are, so to say, his allies and the source from which he derives new strength for asserting himself. Especially if among these comrades there are some who were successful in opposing their perhaps too weak and indulgent parents, and who have been victorious in the struggle for independence, or who have been allowed to adopt some mannerisms of adult life, the adolescent feels that his war against authority is fully justified.

The young people will, however, sometimes lose interest in their comrades, find them bores, feel that their ideas are after all neither so original nor so deep as they thought them, and therefore show a tendency for staying at home and for associating with their family. They are aware, of course, that they have then to "make concessions," as they perhaps will term it, and to adjust themselves somewhat to the rules of common life. Parents very often are deceived by such interludes, which indeed result, not from "the boy having come to his senses," but from the swinging back of his mind to a mild state of introversion which is sure to last but a short time. It would be altogether wrong to begin to "preach at" the youngster on such an occasion, reproaching him for his past behavior and telling him that he now evidently sees what his comrades stood for and how right his parents were. Such an attitude on the part of the parents is probably the surest way of scaring him away again and making him shun his home. It is far better to take things as if all were natural; one may let the youngster see that one is glad at having him more at home; one will do well to let him feel that he is not only welcome but also useful, though it is better to avoid the imposition of tasks he is known to abhor, for instance, because he feels them to be derogatory to his dignity. A boy ought not be asked to do things his father would refuse to do, and a corresponding rule applies to girls.

One ought not to forget that the relations of parents

and children must change with the changing of the latter. Neither the authority which the parents exercised over the children can remain the same after these children have grown to be adolescents, nor can the parents expect to see an adolescent welcome things he used to love when still a child.

There is no doubt that youth stands in need of guidance and accordingly of authority. Nor are the young people themselves ignorant of this fact, since they submit, as has been already remarked, but too readily to any kind of authority, provided it is of their own choice and is not imposed on them by tradition, duty or power. The problem would seem to be, therefore, to make them choose the rightful authority. If they could be induced to accept the authority of those persons who by their position are entitled to exercise it, all would be well; but this is just the difficulty. The revolutionary attitude of the young people, on one hand, and the clumsiness of the parents, on the other, raise an almost unsurmountable barrier to this correct solution.

It will be not without some profit to point out certain common mistakes of parents, whereby they estrange increasingly the minds of the adolescents. It is a very common habit of parents, when they are rebuking an adolescent for some misbehavior, to refer to their own youth and to tell the culprit that they, of course, never did behave that way. This remark is generally quite ineffective. The younger generation does not believe it to be true; and it is not true in most cases. One father remarked to his son of ten years or so:

"Did you ever see me sitting down at table with dirty hands?"

The boy replied: "Well I didn't know you when you were ten years old."

The boy probably was quite right in what he meant to imply. If the young people believe the statements of the parents to be true, they will either pity them for having had such a dull youth and such an uninteresting life, or attribute the fact to the times having been so different when their parents were young. But it may be rather useful to explain to them why one ought not to behave in a certain manner, without referring to one's own excellence.

Another very common mistake consists in taking the parental authority for granted, because it is objectively legitimate. But what is objectively true is not always recognized subjectively as true, even by adults. If we take for granted what our opponent denies, no fruitful discussion will ensue. If we wish to convince another person, we must start from his point of view and lead him gradually on until he realizes his error.

Again, we should clearly recognize that a disturbance of relations between two people is hardly ever the doing of one of them alone; in most cases both of them share in the guilt, though it may be in not quite the same degree. But the misunderstandings which are so extremely frequent between parents and adolescents are mostly caused by the attitude of the former. The adolescent, of course, becomes guilty of many mistakes or even of faults which deserve to be called by stronger names too; but his faults, though materially grave, are not always formally so, since (as has been emphasized already more than once) the adolescent is ignorant of so many things, especially related to his own personality, that he cannot be expected to behave according to objective rules. Instead of holding the young people exclusively responsible, it would be much better if the parents, at least occasionally, reflected on whether they too have made mistakes, and whether they still are making them. They will discover, if they are sufficiently sincere, that they have already been guilty of many blunders, and that of these blunders they are now reaping the harvest. A situation which has been established a long time cannot be changed and reconstructed by a few hours of explanation.

But explanation and the eventual acknowledgment of the mistakes we have made are, after all, the only way which may lead to a reëstablishing of desirable relationships. The adolescent may be very unwilling to recognize authority, but he is generally accessible to reason. If an appeal is made to his own independent reasoning, he may be brought to see the necessity of authority in general and of parental authority in particular. Parental authority is used here, not only for the authority of the parents themselves, but also of all persons invested with such an authority *in loco parentis.*

In all its behavior youth is greatly determined by emotions, by moods, by likings and dislikings, by a variety of "irrational" impulses. But youth is also accessible to reason, and makes use of reason quite frequently when it wishes to criticize the older generation and to prove it to be wrong. This accessibility to reason means, of course, not that one may make a young person see simply by displaying before him all the arguments in favor of one's own and contrary to his position. Reason, even the most convincing, seldom overcomes emotion and mood all of a sudden. It is only by repeated attacks that the fortress of mood may be taken by reason. Inefficient though logic may prove at first and even for quite a long time, it is nevertheless the only means we have at our disposal to make the adolescent "see reason."

Anyone, however, who dares to recommend reason to-day runs the danger of being called a reactionary, of being derided for holding obsolete ideas, and denounced as one who does not understand the signs of the age. Such a person is considered an "intellectualist," and there is no type more bitterly hated by many who believe themselves very "progressive" and exceedingly "modern." These "modern-ists" have raised a war-cry against intellectualism; they preach what they call "irrationalism," and make an alleged overrating of the intellect responsible for the evils of to-day. It is not for these pages to inquire into the eventual truth contained in this accusation. Whether it is partly jus-tified or not, it surely goes much too far in denying all influence to reason and in declaring that reason is not the true guiding light which man has to follow. There is no way of becoming aware of truth other than through reason. Truth is not "felt," and it is not grasped by some mysteri-ous instinctive faculty; it is seen in the cold and clear light of rational analysis.

Nor can it be said that young people, by their very nature, despise reason; if they venture such an assertion, it is because they are told that "intellectualism" belongs to a past age, and that the new times demand not intellect but enthusiasm, not reason but instinct, not speculation but action. No doubt, such a set of ideas appeals to the youthful mind. Instinct, enthusiasm, action as such, independent of specific aims, represent something which suits very well an unclear, nebulous, unripe mentality. Nor is it merely the new times that demand these things; there is to-day but too much of "juvenilism" in the air. It would seem as if the human race to-day consisted, at least in very large part, of unripe minds, capable only of the achievements characteristic of adolescence. It is, of course, a splendid thing to remain young in mind, and if possible in body; but it is definitely wrong to persist in the developmental state of adolescence. Remaining young means retaining the capacity for enjoyment, the vivacity of a man in his mid-twenties, but not the unripeness, the nebulosity, the lack of responsibility and the instability of adolescence. Nobody remains young merely because he still is noisy, lacking in restraint, inclined to all kinds of more or less stupid jokes; he is young in so far as he is, though already advanced in years, able to become interested in new things, has still a good deal of adaptibility, and is capable of freeing himself from prejudices and of adopting new ideas, provided his reason tells him that the latter are right. Many of those who believe themselves to have stayed young are not in the least young minds; their youthfulness consists in being loud, in playing pranks, in enjoying—or believing they enjoy—certain shallow amusements which may be excusable for an adolescent but which are in truth not of the kind to be valued by a ripe personality. What reveals their so-called youth to be altogether artificial and to lack genuineness, is that the "youthful" behavior of such people degenerates no less into mere routine than does the rest of their life.

This cult of youthfulness, which is so marked a characteristic of our times, falsifies the true idea of youth. And it is one additional reason for making the adolescents believe that being young consists mainly in being superficial, in indulging in shallow amusements, in rejecting all that smacks of intellectuality as "snobbish," as "old-fashioned" and "high-brow."

Normal youth is, in fact, as greedy for intellectual satisfaction as it is for all other kinds of satisfaction. The path of the intellect, however, is a steep and difficult one. There is no easy approach to the great problems of life and mind. The intellectual powers of the adolescent mind partake of the general uncertainty. To adventure into the realm of intellectuality may entail a defeat, and defeat is intolerable, because it would seemingly confirm the adolescent's secret misgivings regarding his personal value. The adolescent mind, moreover, somehow feels that there are already enough problems, and it foresees that venturing into intellectuality may end in having to face still more problems. There is an intellectual cowardice as well as a bodily one; but this recoiling from intellectual adventures is, in the case of the adolescent, something we can understand. The adolescent may sometimes be quite willing to become interested in abstract problems of philosophy, politics, and other fields, but he avoids carefully all problems in which his own personality might become involved.

There are, of course, among adolescents as among adults

personalities who are utterly uninterested in all questions of a higher kind; they drudge along at their work because they know that it will enable them to earn a living, or because they realize that they must for the sake of avoiding embarrassing situations; their real interests, however, are in other things, altogether unintellectual. It is not at all sure that these people are really ungifted, but they are definitely unwilling to exert their minds. And they are confirmed in this attitude by general opinion. In following the manifold discussions on education to-day, one becomes aware of a strong tendency against what is termed "academic training," to which "education," on the one hand, and "vocational training," on the other, are opposed. The assumption, however, that education without at least some consideration of intellectuality is possible at all, is of course a grave error which cannot but have disastrous consequences.

The aim of education is the forming of personality and character. The human mind will not act according to approved rules unless these rules are understood. We cannot expect man to form his behavior as a moral person, as a citizen, as a member of society, according to rules which he does not himself acknowledge. And an acknowledging of these rules presupposes an understanding of their ends and of the reasons which underlie them. This understanding is not a matter of instinct, or of "intuition," or of feeling; it is exclusively one of reason. The danger of the coming generations being enthralled by very undesirable ideologies will go on growing, unless reason is reinstated in the dominating position which rightly belongs to it. It is surely wrong to expect great intellectual achievements of everyone. But it is no less a mistake to underrate the intellectual capacity of men. Everything depends on how intellectual things are presented to the minds of the adolescents.

Perhaps a word should be said on the meaning of the terms, "reason" and "intellect." The criticisms of intellectualism rest mostly on a misunderstanding of the term. Intellect or reason, considered objectively, means much more than a mere power of the mind enabling it to grasp abstract notions. According to the psychology of old (that is, of the Scholastics) and to modern researches (which on this point indeed fully confirm the ideas proposed by the medieval scholars, especially by Aquinas), by intellect we must understand the totality of the higher faculties of the human mind. Abstraction or the development of abstract notions is, of course, an achievement of the intellectual faculty. But it is not the only one. Our becoming aware of values is, for instance, due not less to the intellectual activity than is the awareness of truths. Values are not "felt"; they are apprehended by an intellectual operation, and only after the mind has thus got hold of the values do they become capable of arousing feelings. It is true indeed that values which are recognized but "leave us cold" do not usually exercise any notable influence on behavior; but as long as there is no intellectual recognition of values, there is no possibility of their arousing any reaction at all.

The question of intellectuality and of the place to be accorded to intellectual factors in the guidance of adolescents will be taken up once more in the last chapter. What has been said here, had to be emphasized to make clear that reason is a side of human nature which cannot be neglected, unless we are willing to risk a rather one-sided and incomplete development of personality. Adolescence is characterized by the development and change in all faculties of the mind and all sides of personality; no side or feature can be neglected with impunity. The common idea of youth being essentially unintellectual—an idea which indeed is strengthened by the behavior of adolescents—may condition a real crippling of personality. We have heard many an adult complain that the training of his intellect was neglected in his youth, and that he cannot make up for this defect now, having neither the time nor the courage to do so.

There is in human nature a general inclination to follow the "line of least resistance." It is indeed much easier to live up to a level of unintellectuality. And the adolescent mentality is, for reasons which have been pointed out sufficiently, even more inclined to be scared by difficulties. It does not need much intellectual effort to follow a screen play, to read "thrilling" stories, or to keep abreast with the latest events in baseball or tennis. Not even the average interest in technical things can be called intellectual in a higher sense. A real understanding of technique, indeed, demands quite a marked degree of intellectual capacity; but the average interest which young people display in technical things is nearly as shallow as the rest of their inclinations.

Instead of encouraging this tendency towards the superficial and shallow, we ought to try to arouse the slumbering interest of the adolescent in things intellectual. The task is difficult because of the tremendous influence of the general mentality in the opposite direction. A boy who does not display the usual interest in sporting events, or who does not know all about the most famous screen actors, is regarded as crazy, as priggish, and as being behind his time.

This general mentality, together with the uncertainty of his mind and his natural tendency to follow the line of least resistance, contributes towards making the adolescent feel that many things, especially of the intellect, are "away above him." This often-heard phrase sounds to some as being the expression of modest self-knowledge, or as being the expression of the "new spirit" which discards all "unnecessary" speculation and concentrates only on the useful and practical. But the phrase is commonly the expression of discouragement and of cowardice. It is the attitude of the fox who found the grapes too sour because he could not reach them. And this attitude is, of course, strengthened by the fear of becoming an object of critical remarks, of being regarded as "high-brow" by one's comrades and of being dropped by them because of not sharing their interests. These are very powerful factors with an adolescent, and to counteract them may prove quite a problem.

"But how can I," some parent will ask, "arouse intellectual interests in my adolescent children, when I myself have not been trained in that way, because I was not interested in such things" (or because of lack of opportunity)? While this question may seem to raise an unsurmountable obstacle, such is not actually the case. Nobody will expect a man whose whole life has been given to working for his family to discuss problems of metaphysics with his boy; if only the boy is not told that all these things are nonsense and if he is not already too deeply discouraged, he will find someone to talk to. But every father may be supposed to know things to discuss with his boy, things which are not just the most trivial facts of daily life. There is, for instance, politics. Many political discussions indeed consist merely in cursing the party one does not belong to, or in criticizing the current administration, or suchlike things. Political discussion between son and father becomes moreover easily fruitless and even something still worse, if the father will not listen to the boy's ideas, deeming them immature (as probably they are) and not worth considering. Maybe they are not worth considering, but the boy himself is. The usual tone of such discussions is indeed not at all what one would wish it to be for the sake of the boy. He is nearly sure to develop political ideas other than those his father holds, partly out of opposition to the older generation, and partly because of the change political conceptions undergo in the course of the years. A father who declares his boy's ideas to be nonsense merely because they are not his own, is sure to alienate the mind of his son more and more. But he could help the boy if he would condescend to listen, to argue, to ask questions; by asking the boy to explain and prove his views, the father may not only stimulate the intellectual interest in his boy, but also make him feel on better terms with his father, and thus gradually bridge the gap separating the two. What has been said here of political discussions applies of course, *mutatis mutandis*, to all other questions too.

Such behavior of a parent will also do much in lessening the general discouragement of the adolescent personality. Encouragement is something of which the adolescents are urgently in need. They do not seem, as a rule, to be discouraged; nor are they always. But every adolescent is subject, at least at times, to fits of despondency and of discouragement. This is, of course, very detrimental to moral development. The feeling that they never will overcome certain difficulties, never be able to realize certain ideals, etc., works as a heavy weight drawing them down to lower levels. Discouragement is the necessary consequence of uncertainty, especially of uncertainty about the "self." Adolescents feel this "self" to be unreliable, because it is so changing, because it is still so strange and slips, as it were, between their fingers whenever they try to get hold of it.

Success has a definitely encouraging influence. But not all success amounts to general encouragement. Many a youngster may feel proud of his successes in sport and go on feeling discouraged in regard to other things. Things that a man (whether still an adolescent or already an adult) does not feel capable of doing, are generally not attempted. But nobody can, in truth, foretell whether he will be able to do a thing unless he tries. The words, "I cannot," are often but an euphemistic way of saying: "I will not." While, on the one hand, ambition is a strong stimulus towards achievement or attempted achievement, it may become, on the other hand, a very serious handicap.

Ambition is usually not content with moderate successes, but longs for great ones. Great successes, however, are not to be had so easily; they are either for the genius, or are the result of long training and strenuous endeavor. Even the genius himself cannot dispense with exertion. Goethe, exaggerating a truth into a paradox, once said: "Genius is industry." Long-continued endeavor, without immediate and visible success, is repugnant to the general mentality of the adolescent. The future indeed looms large in his life; but it is a still indistinct and vague future, for the sake of which he is loath to undertake a work of doubtful success. The adolescent, being uncertain of himself, needs repeated success to strengthen his self-confidence; when he knows or has found out already that he cannot achieve such successes as he craves for, there is a danger that he will give up all endeavor for higher aims. We have, accordingly, to avoid discouraging the adolescent beyond the degree already natural for his age.

But we cannot, because this is contrary to nature, procure for the adolescent great successes. And to make him believe that he has already achieved such successes would be a deception and would cause damage, instead of rendering a real help. Even if we feel sure that we have to deal with an unusually gifted youngster (maybe a genius), we ought to be careful in expressing our appreciation of his doings. Here too we have to adhere to the middle course, not discouraging the adolescent by telling him that his achievements are nothing, nor letting him believe that he has already attained the summit.

The wisest course is to make the young people see that

they have to content themselves at first with smaller
achievements. But if one tells them so flatly and refers them
to the future, they may feel discouraged. They want to be
great and important and successful right now; they cannot
wait for the realization of a future of which they have but
a very dim idea, and which scares them at least as much as
it attracts them. How indeed can they be expected to have
a clearer idea of the future, when they have but a very
blurred notion of the present? Encouragement to be effective has to apply to actual things.

The task of encouragement has two sides, a negative and
a positive one. One must beware of discouraging the
adolescent. One ought, therefore, never to rebuke him for
something wrong he has done, without letting him feel
that one trusts in his capacity to behave differently. One
has to be very careful especially with a youngster who has
just become submerged in a fit of despondency. During
such a fit an adolescent does not necessarily seem depressed
or sad or sluggish; he may, on the contrary, appear impudent and restive and disobedient, and create the impression
of being but too sure of himself. It never suffices to consider one single feature of behavior; one must always take
into account the total behavior. This constitutes indeed a
serious difficulty; the complexity of modern life makes it
nearly impossible for one person to observe another in all
the different situations which make up his life. The only
exception is life in a boarding school; but even there many
sides of an individual's behavior may escape the attention
of the supervisors. Ordinarily, the parents do not know
how the boy and the girl behave when they are with their

comrades, nor what they do while in the classroom; the teacher does not know of the behavior at home or on the playground; the confessor does not know anything beyond what his penitents tell him. But a close observation will reveal to the trained eye little traits disclosing things which do not come to the surface in one particular situation.

A person may behave very differently in different situations. This does not mean that he has "no character," but that to him the differences which the observer perhaps feels to be negligible are very important. A boy may be embarrassed in school, altogether normal on the playground, and impudent at home. This may be because he resents the critical attitude of the teacher and the class, feels at his ease with the team, and has found out that he can impose on his parents and thus bolster his sense of superiority. There may be other reasons; but a closer investigation will always show that character is a unit, and that the apparent contradictions resulting from the variations of attitude are due to the ideas which the adolescent— or, for that matter, every man—has of the various situations.

The guidance and influencing of adolescents is not an easy task. But it can be accomplished if we first become aware of the characteristics of the personality we have to form. There are certain features of behavior, some of them generally considered as faults, which reveal more of the deeper structure of personality than is commonly believed. But the educator has to beware carefully of assuming the attitude of the judge; his principal task is not to condemn, but to understand. Condemnation may prove an efficient means of influencing, if it is used with discretion; so may punishment. But both presuppose thorough understanding.

Chapter IV

Some Special Features

THE GENERAL REMARKS of the foregoing chapters are very much in need of illustration by special instances. It is, of course, impossible for a manual such as this to give a complete list of all the many shades and varieties of behavior which become either a problem to the educator or an opportunity for discovering the true nature of his pupil's mental make-up. It will be possible only to cite some striking and particularly instructive features of adolescent behavior.

One point of great and general importance must be emphasized. No feature of behavior or of character can be interpreted according to one set pattern. There is "no dictionary of symptoms." The same feature may have a different signification in different personalities. It may have even a different signification in the selfsame personality at different times and in different situations. We are, moreover, too much inclined to speak of the "same" feature and to disregard certain slight, but nevertheless significant, shades. What to the casual observer appears to be the "same" kind of behavior may be in truth something quite different; we may reproach a man, of whatever age, for behaving quite differently in what we feel to be the "same" situation, and overlook the fact that to him the two situations in question are not identical at all; we may get the impression that some youngster is just copying another or an adult person, because we do not see any difference, and the behavior may spring from quite different sources.

Notwithstanding this general rule, we may rely on certain interpretations of more or less typical forms of behavior. We may rely on our interpretation all the more when we feel that the behavior springs from the very basic structure of adolescent mentality. The reliability of our interpretations becomes greater still, the nearer the phenomenon approaches to abnormality. It is much easier to develop a typology of abnormal characters than of normal ones. It is rather significant that the first modern attempts at establishing a typology of human personalities were made by physicians. One pathological personality indeed resembles another of the same kind much more closely than one normal person resembles another. There is no "originality" at all in abnormal features; only normal people have originality. In describing and analyzing certain "symptoms," which are not truly abnormal but not quite normal either, we do not run much risk of doing violence to reality and substituting preconceived ideas for facts.

The meaning given here to the term of "normality" needs elucidation. Normality means "conformity with a norm"; but our norm here is not that of the average, not the arithmetical mean, but the norm of the ideal. Even if, in some country, 99% of the inhabitants were affected with tuberculosis, the 1% free from the disease would represent normality. Even if some feature of behavior is observed in the great majority, it does not become normal unless it corresponds to the true idea of human nature.

Some few words may be permitted on this true idea of

human nature. The nature of a thing is determined by its highest qualities, by those which distinguish it from others of a lower level. The essence of plants is not determined by their being built up of elements which we find also in inanimate nature, but by their being capable of growth, of reproduction, of assimilation—achievements which are unknown in the realm of dead matter. The animal is what it is, not because of the qualities which it has in common with the plant, but because of those which raise its nature above that of plants—because of its capacity of local movement, spontaneity, sensory perception, purposive instinctive behavior. Thus, man is not to be defined as an animal, unless the peculiar feature of rationality is added. To attempt to develop an adequate idea of man's nature by considering first and principally the features common to man and beast, is tantamount to misunderstanding human nature absolutely; not what man may achieve as well as a beast characterizes human nature, but what he alone can do and no beast can ever achieve. Intellectual understanding, moral behavior, and cultural progress are features characteristic of human nature, but not instincts or drives and longings originating in the lower faculties of the human person. A man is the more human, the more he is alive to the peculiar tasks and problems conditioned by the higher faculties he has been given. The closer some activity approaches to mere vital function, the less human it becomes.

What is normal and what not, though it might be extremely common, is determined then by this idea of norm. Certain features of behavior are quite common in adoles-

cence, but, because of this, they may not be called normal
ones. And in view of their being "abnormal," they are
susceptible of a more or less uniform interpretation. But
we have, in spite of this, to bear in mind that they assume
an individual note according to the personality to which
they belong. Even in the level of bodily symptoms there
is such a determining influence of individuality; the
"same" disease is not quite identical in Peter and in Paul.

The "abnormal" features which we are going to analyze
here have been chosen for two reasons: they reveal more
of the particular structure of the adolescent mind than do
many others, and they become often rather serious problems in education.

Embarrassment or bashfulness is found very frequently
in young people. If reactions or attitudes of this nature are
more marked, they are felt, by those suffering from them
and by third persons, to be definitely abnormal. Another
feature which one may well group with the two mentioned
is timidity, though there is quite a difference here, since
in timidity a feeling of anxiety is the primary element,
whereas this emotion is secondary in bashfulness and embarrassment.

Embarrassment or bashfulness and timidity are believed
to be "natural" in certain situations; but being natural does
not mean that they are inevitable. It is noteworthy that
these reactions were thought of differently in different
ages. There was a time, and it was not long ago either, when
a young person (especially a girl) was supposed to be embarrassed and bashful under certain circumstances; not to
feel so—or at least not to behave as if she felt so—was

definitely discreditable. But bashfulness is no longer considered a sign of a well-educated person who "knows his station." This kind of behavior is, therefore, not the necessary effect of some objective situation; it is rather the outcome of a subjective attitude.

The less desirable embarrassment is, or the more shameful it is adjudged to be, the more strongly will a person strive to react against this state and to conceal it behind some other behavior. Embarrassment does not show itself always in its true guise; it may be masked by garrulity, impertinence, arrogance, or some other feature of behavior which apparently is its very opposite. Because a person desires so intensely that his embarrassment shall pass unnoticed, he overdoes his attempts to hide it. The forwardness of young people is often much less due to their being really conceited and fully convinced of their importance than to the attempt to disguise their exact feelings. Here we have an example of the often discussed process of "overcompensation," which one must bear in mind if one wants to understand the otherwise often unintelligible behavior of adolescents, both boys and girls.

This overcompensation is, as everyone sees, due to the desire to make a better impression than one would by being bashful and embarrassed. This very same wish is, though unknown to the subject himself, already at work in the conditioning of his embarrassment and timidity. These behavior types, and several others too, may be said to spring from an ambiguous basic structure; they are the result and the expression of cowardice combined with ambition. If the bashful person were indifferent to the impression he is going to make, he would not behave or feel as he does. Embarrassment indeed implies the idea—whether conscious or not—of the situation being very important; embarrassed people act as if the most unimportant fact (their casual meeting of a stranger, for instance) were to become a decisive influence in their lives. Timidity, like all feelings akin to anxiety, implies the idea of danger; where there is no danger, no sentiment resembling fear can arise. The danger and the importance of the situation, however, consist in just this: the fear of not making as good an impression as the person really wants to make. It is not difficult to see why this kind of behavior is so common in adolescents. They are never sure of making a good impression, because they are not sure of themselves and of their representing a real value.

People are, of course, quite right in wanting to make a good impression; they should desire to do so for their own sake as well as for the sake of others. It is, no doubt, much more agreeable to meet a person whom we may like and appreciate than one we feel to be repulsive. In so far as the wish to make a good impression is born from the consideration of the feelings of our neighbors, it is definitely right. But we cannot expect to make a good impression always and on everyone; to cherish such a hope is certainly overdoing things and springs from a secret overrating of one's own personality, or, at least, from the secret wish to be an exceptionally valuable personality. This exaggerated idea of one's own self, however, is associated in the minds of adolescents—and of all people sharing their emotions—with a secret doubt of their having any value; the result is embarrassment.

There may be situations in which almost anyone would feel more or less embarrassed. We may well feel so when we have to meet a man whom we deem to be very superior, whom we greatly admire, or on whose opinion of us much depends. But the main characteristic of habitually embarrassed people is that they are embarrassed even when there is manifestly no reason for feeling this emotion.

Embarrassment disappears when the person "feels at home"; that is, when he feels that he is sufficiently appreciated. There would be no embarrassment at all, if the individual felt that he would be appreciated in any case. The exaggerated tendency to embarrassment denotes, accordingly, a correspondingly strong longing for appreciation. This longing is unreasonable, because it expects success from the very first moment, and is unwilling to make the effort necessary to attain success.

This habit is painful for the person afflicted with it, and also for those who observe it. It might seem, therefore, that embarrassment and similar behavior traits have but negative qualities. But in examining the situation more closely one becomes aware that this is not quite true. Because of its annoyance to both sides, embarrassment becomes a good excuse; bashfulness gives rise to the presumption that there is "more behind" the bashful person, and that his clumsiness or mistakes are due merely to this habit. People meeting an embarrassed person will think him to be probably much better than he appears, that he could do much better work than he actually accomplishes, etc. The habit of bashfulness implies in truth: "I long to make a tremendous impression, but not being sure of doing so and not content to put up with less, I shelter behind this behavior which hides my true feelings and which, at the same time, supplies a valid excuse in case I should prove a failure." Not that the person himself is conscious of these thoughts; he is absolutely unaware of them, at least as a rule, though there may be some moments in which he gets a glimpse of the truth—from which, of course, he looks away as quickly as possible. But this last habit is not the prerogative of just bashful or juvenile personalities; it is pretty common with all of us.

The overweening aspirations of such a person—though he entertains them rather unconsciously—are even more easily detected in other states of "inhibition" and anxiety, as, for instance, in the confusion which seizes a person when he has to answer questions or to pass an examination. It is quite remarkable that these senseless attacks of fear in examinations usually befall students who have worked rather strenuously; one who has done but little work, has to keep his head cool, since this is his only chance. These characteristics become particularly visible in oral examinations. The state of fear, benumbing the intellectual faculties, does not help the student, but it may serve as a plausible excuse in case of failure or of a not quite brilliant success. After having failed to pass his examination a certain boy remarked: "It was not I who failed; it was my over-anxiety." A person whose ambition is kept within reasonable limits is satisfied with having passed his examination and having done his work. Overstrung ambition is satisfied only by a striking success; but such a success depends on several factors, some of which are independent of the student's personality and make the result uncertain. A success less than the best possible amounts, in the mind of the over-ambitious, to defeat.

This kind of aberration is not seldom observed in adolescents. But they may develop also another attitude which, though apparently the opposite of the first, is nevertheless due to the very same causes. They may become quite indifferent to success in school; what marks they get are immaterial to them; whether they pass an examination or not is of no consequence. But there are in truth very few in whom this attitude is genuine. It is generally but an assumed pose, a kind of rôle played, though the students are not aware that they feel quite differently in the depth of their minds. This apparent indifference is again partly the attitude of the fox towards the allegedly sour grapes; partly it is a kind of protective mechanism defending the but too vulnerable ambition against disappointment.

It is not always easy to cure a person from this tendency to unreasonable fear. Sometimes indeed it is sufficient to tell him that his task is not to be brilliant or to make an unprecedented record; he may then become conscious of his hitherto unnoticed longing for such a success. Although it is not sure that this knowledge alone will suffice to eradicate his unfortunate habit, a recognition of its true nature is the indispensable beginning of the campaign to cure it.

One has, of course, to guard carefully against all influences which might tend to strengthen such a habit and cause it to sprout still deeper roots. Very often the extravagant ambition did not originate in the adolescent himself, but has been inculcated by others, usually by his parents.

There are parents who want their children to be brilliant, primarily for the sake of gratifying their own vanity or for the sake of seeing their children attain objectives which they themselves were not able to realize. But this is not the task of children; they are not born just to gratify their parents' vanity. They have to live their own lives, to do the things they are meant for, to achieve what they are capable of, to realize the potentialities of their nature. Overexacting parents, even if they are impelled by a misunderstood sense of duty, are as much of a nuisance and a danger as are too lenient parents who admire whatever their children do and are incapable of ever finding fault with them. The first shatter the courage of their offspring, and the second neglect to develop it.

The uncertainty which pervades the whole being of the adolescent makes him, without his understanding his own behavior, either seek for excuses if he should fail to achieve what he secretly aspires to, or avoid all situations which contain the threat of eventual defeat. Adolescents are greatly inclined to confuse the notions of success and achievement—or, on the other hand, those of failure and defeat. Not that this confusion is characteristic of adolescence alone; quite a few older people make the same mistakes. But these older people have, perhaps, retained a little too much of the juvenile attitudes. There are many modes of behavior which may ensure either excuse or avoidance. There is, for instance, a kind of laziness and a kind of dullness which have really nothing to do with a lack of the will for work or of intelligence; they are merely habits built up for the sake of avoiding situations which might eventually involve a defeat. It is not possible to analyze here the many kinds of apparent and real laziness and dullness; but it is well to emphasize that these notions cover attitudes of very different origin and nature. It is a serious mistake to consider all lazy children or adolescents as having the "same" defect, or all dull children as being just a little above morons.

The physical state of the adolescent, be it remarked incidentally, may play a great rôle in the conditioning of certain features of behavior, although the mental factors are doubtless much more influential. One cannot deny, however, that the physical state may determine certain variations of mental activity. Many a child and adolescent has indeed been rebuked or even punished for things which did not depend at all on his good or bad will, but which resulted exclusively from bodily factors. All kinds of bodily troubles, especially chronic disturbances, may have certain reactions on mental functions and on behavior. A physical examination is advisable in every case involving serious difficulties in education.

"Nervousness," however, definitely does not belong to these physical troubles. The notion of "weak nerves" must be discarded altogether from this category; the nervous system as an anatomical and physiological unit is, even in a "nervous" person, quite in order. We know that the behavior and the "nervous" symptoms in such a person may be changed much by mental treatment; but there is no chance of ever changing the state of the nervous system by persuasion, suggestion, analysis, or what not. We may have, however, every reason for attributing some trouble in behavior to purely mental causes, but we are never quite sure that there are no physical factors. Before attributing slackness, despondency, incapacity for work, lack of concentration, etc., to merely mental causes, one will do well first to have the adolescent examined thoroughly by a physician.

A feature which is very common in adolescents, and which is often the occasion of great trouble to the educator, is instability of mood and of behavior in general. Some words have already been said on this matter; some few remarks may be added. It is wrong to consider this instability, unpleasant though it may be, simply as a fault and to attribute it to factors over which the adolescent has full control. This behavior indeed springs from sources unknown to the individual and beyond his influence. The instability is, in truth, the rather inevitable result of uncertainty. A man who is uncertain about the way he has to take will repeatedly turn first to one side and then to the other, before he can make up his mind. The greater the uncertainty is, the longer this state of doubt and of oscillation between the various possible ways will last. As has been pointed out more than once, the adolescent is uncertain not only about the ways—that is, about reality—but also about himself. The world shows another face, so to say, every day, and the "ego" looking at this world is equally inconstant. This being the case, one should really not wonder at the adolescent being unstable and changing his mind so often. He may be interested in his work today, because he feels equal to it, and lapse into indifference to-morrow, because he has lost the feeling of ability to achieve. He may understand something to-day, and not understand it to-morrow, because he has become another person overnight. It is no wonder, then, that the adolescent tires so often of some work which he had just undertaken with remarkable enthusiasm. The same reason is not seldom the root of the often deplored unreliability of young people. They will promise something, and not keep their promise; they will be apparently ready to do something, and immediately forget it; they will seem quite convinced by some explanation given to them, and act the next day as if they never had heard anything of the kind. This is not necessarily the result of any real immorality, or of neglect of moral obligation, or of a lack of consideration, etc. It may as well be just the consequence of the young personality having become different, so that the reasons which were felt to be convincing but a short time before have become stale and unimpressive, having lost their solidity. To different states of mind correspond different arguments, or rather different ways of presenting the same truths. A chain of thought which may be convincing to a highly cultured man of our day might have been altogether unconvincing to a contemporary of Coriolanus, and what impressed the medieval mind most seems futile to many people of modern times. What applies to the history of mankind, applies also to the history of individual persons.

The behavior of instability, however, offers a point of attack. It would be wrong merely to rebuke an adolescent for his lack of reliability; if he is not shown the causes of his behavior, he will not be improved by listening to reproaches. He knows, of course, that promises have to be kept; he knows too that there is no exception for him. He is not so well aware that there are many other rules equally binding. He may doubt quite often whether there exists any really binding rule. This doubt is aggravated by his own instability; a person who can rely so little on himself, is easily led to doubt the reliability of anything whatever. There are, of course, other influences too; the general idea of the "relativity of values" (of certain things having been true until now and not being true any more), the enormous differences between what various people declare to be right, etc., cannot but increase the uncertainty and, directly as well as indirectly, the doubting attitude of the adolescent in regard to rules and laws.

But though the adolescent knows of his obligations (at least of some of them) in a rather vague and general way, he feels that in neglecting them he is not quite so guilty as his judge believes him to be. This feeling is not based on a clear idea of what prompted his behavior; it is but a dim awareness of there having entered into play factors he is unable to control. His subjective feelings, new and strange as they are, have a much greater influence on his behavior than objective considerations. This fact has to be made clear to him. The adolescent is quite capable of seeing that subjective feelings have but little weight in comparison to objective necessities. He will understand this easily, if he is shown that human life is ruled first of all by objective laws. He will understand also that such laws have to exist if mankind is to hold its own against the destructive forces of nature and (if he were relieved of all restraint) of man himself. But it is not enough to know of the existence of these laws and of their special content. Laws may be known, and nevertheless become the object of aversion and of revolt. What man has to learn, and what he is best taught while still a youngster, is that these laws, which are apparently outside of himself and forcing him to obedience, are in truth the very laws of his own existence and his own personality. They are not merely some strange powers one cannot help but obey, because otherwise they would destroy us; they are the very basis of individual human existence. The laws of reality are at the same time the laws of each individual, since the individual is part of this reality and not merely opposed to it. Rebellion against these laws therefore undermines the individual's very existence. The idea that self-assertion necessarily involves opposition or rebellion must be combatted. It is one of the most disastrous mistakes the human mind ever became guilty of, because it destroys the true conception of man's place in the totality of real being.

The adolescent will readily concede that human society cannot persist without honesty and reliability prevailing in it. Even the revolutionary, even the communist and the anarchist, however critical they may feel towards the existing society and its morals, cannot deny that rules must be observed if mankind and society are to exist at all. We may disregard the objection that there is no need for humanity to exist, because this idea will hardly be defended seriously even by an adolescent, though he might use it just for the sake of scoring a point in debate. He will generally concede that reliability and honesty are necessary. He might restrict this obligation, and feel that such behavior is

necessary only within a certain circle or set; one meets indeed quite frequently young people who will not recoil
from any kind of dishonest or even criminal action, who
do not mind cheating or stealing, but who will behave in
a scrupulously honest way towards the members of their
own gang. It ought not to be too difficult to make them
see that the laws they accept among their "set" must regu-
late all kinds of relations between men.

The problem of the criminal or anti-social adolescent,
however, has some special features; it cannot be discussed
here, since we are occupied only with the average and normal adolescent. The latter must be led to understand that
and why he does not live up to his own principles, or to
those which he cannot but acknowledge as justified and
necessary. The point is that, in dealing with the adolescent,
we have first of all to help him to some understanding of
himself. We may safely presume that he somehow knows
his behavior to be wrong, and that at the same time he
feels it to be not quite so wrong as it appears to the eyes
of the adult moralist. It is well, it is even very necessary,
to discuss the moral aspect of the adolescent's behavior;
but there are doubtless many ways of asserting the claims
of morality. Little is gained by simply telling the adolescent
what he ought to do and how he ought to behave, because
he knows this pretty well himself. The important thing is
to make him see, and if possible to discover for himself,
why he does not do what in his own eyes is right. The best
way is to let him find out; we ought to make him explain
why he acted just as he has done and does. He is sure
to have quite a number of reasons for his behavior. By

analyzing these reasons, he may be brought to understand that they are not as valid as he believed them to be.

Situations in which the adolescent knows himself guilty, and expects to be punished or at least rebuked, may be employed to great advantage for establishing closer contact with him if they are carefully handled. By explaining to the culprit that one cannot but disapprove of his behavior and that one has to punish it (at least, to condemn the deed), and at the same time telling him that one wishes to understand his motives, one may not seldom pierce through the armor of reticence and of stubbornness which the sensitive soul has donned.

But mere condemnation or punishment without any explanation or any attempt at understanding will probably but reinforce the attitude of revolt. Punishment in education is not the same thing as it is in penal law. The law punishes the deed; in education and in moral guidance we have to consider very carefully the motives and the general mentality of the culprit. It may be even with an adolescent, as it is very often with children, that he did not quite realize the true nature of his deed; to punish someone for something he did not know to be bad or as bad as it objectively is, would be a very great mistake which cannot but increase the distance between the young person and the educator. To diminish this distance is, however, one of our most important tasks, since this is an indispensable condition for gaining the necessary influence and authority over the adolescent.

Discussions of their point of view with adolescents and our attempts to prove it to be wrong are often highly unsuccessful at first. Stubbornness and unwillingness to see another's point of view, the more or less arrogant upholding of their own ideas and similar traits, are very common in adolescents. Stubbornness in face of objectively convincing ideas is always a sign of an exaggerated and vulnerable ambition. Only a person who has to defend his position at any cost, because relinquishing it would be tantamount to defeat and to acknowledging that he is really of no consequence, will try to uphold ideas he himself feels to be indefensible. When he finds that he cannot rely on reasons, he may try to avail himself of more or less sophistic arguments; but if these too prove useless, there remains but the way of stubbornness, of impenetrability, of apparent lack of understanding, of outbreaks of temperament, in which some insignificant detail is emphasized which supplies a pretext for becoming angry. He may, of course, also resort to the strategy of becoming suddenly uninterested, of giving but perfunctory answers, or of assenting without any inner conviction; adolescents have a trick of saying yes, while letting the other person see that he has not made any real impression and that the assent is made only for the sake of getting rid of an annoying situation. In such discussions, therefore, one has to be careful of what one says, and not to give the adolescent an opportunity of evading the issue. If he tries to fly off at a tangent, one has to bring him back, firmly but without wounding his susceptibility, to the matter under discussion.

In telling the young people that they are mistaken in their ideas or acting contrary to their own knowledge, one ought not to start with stern reproofs and hurl at their heads the accusation that they are wrong in their ideas and perverted in their characters. Even less ought one to indulge in gloomy predictions regarding the life on which an adolescent is embarking: "If you go on this way, you will end by becoming a criminal." Such words as these (but too often used by parents) and other similar prophecies will make the worst possible impression; they will but strengthen the young person's feeling of uncertainty and his distrust in his own capacities. Nor ought one to threaten him with very stern measures in case of the repetition of his misbehavior, unless one is fully determined to put them into execution. Threats which are not executed lose all efficacy, and weaken definitely all authority. By assuming the attitude of the judge (who has to be necessarily aloof), instead of letting the offender know that he still is cared for and the object of love, one will never draw closer to his person. But one ought, on the other hand, to beware of all exaggerated sentimentality. Unimpassioned and objective discussion is generally more impressive than complaints and sentimental scenes.

We cannot expect the adolescent to be visibly impressed by our words. If he is, the reaction will not last long. If his behavior has been proved to be wrong and if he is not capable of finding any answer, he will often retire into sullen silence. This behavior is not seldom taken as a sign of offensiveness and of depravity; parents will regard the adolescent as obdurate and hopeless; his relapsing into the very faults he himself acknowledged to be wrong is considered as a sign of bad will and of his being, so to say, incurable. These interpretations, however, may be altogether mistaken. Sullenness and silence may be the effect of deeply wounded feelings and of a pride which forbids all expression. Relapsing into the very same faults may be due to the fact that the young mind despairs of ever overcoming certain inclinations. It may be due to other reasons, too. A boy, for instance, has been shown that things he used to do together with his comrades are bad or at least undesirable; but it is perhaps expecting too much that he will resist the temptation coming from these comrades and resist also their jeering and gibing. All these influences, and particularly the inner situation of the adolescent mind, have to be taken into consideration.

The effect of these discussions will be less critical, if the adolescent's wrongdoing is not the only occasion for starting them. If the parents have accustomed the young people to talk to them on various and as a rule rather impersonal topics, the discussion of a personal matter will not be such an exceptional event. If such a conversation takes place only for the sake of educational ends, the adolescent will assume an attitude of defense the moment he sees what is coming. It is evident that such a situation may become a handicap for the educational endeavors.

If one should tell a sulking and reticent youngster that one knows perfectly how he feels, no great progress will be made. In the first place, he will not believe it, because he holds the older generation incapable of understanding his mind; he will moreover resent such a remark, since he is anxiously striving not to reveal his feelings, and will therefore be spurred to a still more energetic attempt to hide them. Since hiding his feelings may become very difficult, it is but natural that he will come to wish that he had not these feelings at all. And it is not a too difficult task to cast out of one's consciousness things one does not want to find there. We did not need the discoveries, or alleged discoveries, of psychoanalysis to make us acquainted with "repression." Years before psychoanalysis appeared on the scene, the fact of its existence had been stated very clearly by Frederick Nietzsche. Poets always knew of this curious power of the mind, nor was it altogether unknown to the moralists. But since this name has come to be accepted, let us continue to call this mental operation "repression." If we act in such a way as to make repression desirable to the adolescent, we shall achieve just the opposite of what we wish to realize. What has been repressed has not only disappeared from consciousness; it also becomes a barrier which hinders similar things from entering into the consciousness, and conditions an automatic mechanism of defense. The same adolescent whom we found easy to convince and ready to follow our line of thought, may because of this consequence of repression prove on the next occasion impenetrable, unwilling to see our point of view, either glibly evading arguments or answering them with fits of temperament. Under such circumstances, it is much better not to say anything, but to act on the basis of our knowledge of the adolescent's reaction.

In such a case, as in several others too, it is often a good way not to mention the individual case at all, but to introduce the problem occasionally in a general and, as it were, theoretical manner. If one can get the adolescent to tell of some of his friends and comrades and of their behavior, one might eventually try to analyze these things—of course, without becoming offensive or simply condemning these other young people—and point out some general rules or motives which prompt such a behavior. One need not—one had indeed better not—make any personal allusion. It is probable that the adolescent will draw the necessary conclusions by himself.

Among the reasons the adolescent will eventually give for his behavior is one which generally meets but little belief, though it is in many instances quite true. Many adolescents feel that they are utterly incapable of behaving as they ought; they are not wrong, in a way, because they feel themselves so little reliable. They feel that it is in truth useless to promise this or that, because the one who promises will not be the one who is expected to keep the promise. It is not only other people who cannot rely on the promises of an adolescent; he himself is fully aware of the fact that his resolutions are not worth very much. But this is not a sign of bad character; it is the symptom of a character not yet developed and even less stabilized.

Because of this, and of many other facts which we have already mentioned repeatedly, the adolescent is easily discouraged. There is always the danger of this discouragement increasing to a point where he loses all hope of doing good. Callous though he may seem, he usually appreciates that he has become a sorrow and a care to his parents, even if he is not told so. Some children, many adolescents, and not a few adults behave badly because they have given up all hope, and because they simply despair of ever being able to behave well. Despair and discouragement are very often at the bottom of misbehavior. "Many sins are done out of weakness, but few spring really from malice," St. Augustine says somewhere. This is particularly true of the adolescent; and his weakness is perhaps easier to understand and to condone than delinquencies of which so many grown-up people become guilty.

The adolescent must be shown that it is quite right to strive for a high and lofty goal, but that to realize such a goal demands the exercise of patience. The young mind is essentially impatient; it seeks not only success, but immediate success, and it deems delay an equivalent of defeat. The older generation tells the younger that one must be patient, that achievements need time, that one has to bide one's opportunity, that one has to prepare carefully. But the young people, when listening to such a lecture, believe only that the adults have become tired, that they have lost the fine *élan* of youth, that they are discouraged and despondent, and that it will be for the next generation, their own, to keep alive this energy, this aggressiveness, which they believe they possess. But youth, only too often, expends its energy on things not worthy of enthusiasm. Youth easily takes this sentiment itself for the thing that matters; youth is essentially subjectivistic in its attitudes. This subjectivism becomes an important factor in two great problems which education in adolescence has to grapple with: daydreaming and sexuality. Because of certain peculiarities adhering to these things and because of their importance, it is necessary to devote to them a separate chapter.

CHAPTER V

Daydreams and Sexuality

SOME READERS will perhaps wonder at seeing daydreams and sexuality linked together. Even though they
are aware that sexual elements enter a good deal into daydreams, and that daydreaming very often accompanies
sexual feelings, they may not regard this as a sufficient
reason for establishing a close connection between these
two phenomena. Now, it is true that daydreaming is something apart from sexuality, and that sexuality has an origin
of its own which has nothing to do with daydreams. It is
true also that the connection between the two may appear
as purely accidental. But there is, in truth, so close a connection between them, especially when we consider the
psychology of adolescence, that the discussion of these two
phenomena under one and the same head is certainly
justifiable. The nature of this connection will become clear
in the course of the discussion.

The emergence of sexual desire and the attaining of
sexual maturity have been always considered as a prominent feature in adolescence. It has been emphasized already that it is a mistake to regard sexuality and its development as the pivotal fact in adolescence, notwithstanding its undoubted importance and its prominent rôle during this age. To repeat it once more, the very central fact
is the consolidation of the definitive ego or self and the

person's gradually becoming conscious of this self, of its peculiarities, and of its uniqueness.

Sexual desires arise because of physiological reasons. Normal development of the human organism brings about, at the age of adolescence, the maturing of sexuality, the development of sexual function, and the bodily changes characteristic of maturity. Though the bodily processes are undoubtedly the cause of sexual experiences, sexual sensations and sexual desires, it is entirely too simple a view to limit the study of sexuality to the bodily side and to regard the mental phenomena as mere reflexes of the bodily changes. Human nature is not of such a structure as to allow so simple an explanation. The mental states corresponding to sexuality, the longings which draw the two sexes together, the love which may spring up in their hearts, are not mere effects of bodily processes. The materialist may indeed hold such views; but, to do so, he must shut his eyes to very obvious facts. One who sees in the relations of the sexes only the physiological factor and its immediately correlated mental phenomena (the craving for satisfaction and the propensity to lust), misses some very essential elements. There is also love apart from sexuality; in fact, the narrowmindedness of certain "psychologies"—*lucus a non lucendo*—which try to "explain" all kinds of love as being derived from sexuality, cannot withstand the impact of plain facts.

The belief that bodily sexuality is sufficient to explain all the complicated mental states involved in the relations of the sexes is indeed a remnant of the "nothing-else-but-mentality" of the nineteenth century, which hoped to explain all, even the most subtle and most lofty, sentiments as the mere results of bodily and ultimately of physical and chemical processes. This hope, which was nonsensical even at the time of its inception, has been completely dispelled. There are, of course, still many who have not been able to free themselves from the fetters of this materialistic mentality. But psychology as a whole is undoubtedly developing towards a truer conception. It has been the error of modern psychology not to have devoted sufficient attention to pure description, and to have cherished excessively the idea of making the study of the human mind something like applied physics. Psychology, as it developed during the nineteenth century (at the middle of which it came first into existence as an independent discipline), was fashioned according to the tenets of material science. It was, accordingly, incapable of grasping the essentials of its own subject. Only in recent years has there developed a psychology which really deserves to be called by this name.

Freudian psychology, with its quite unwarranted exaggeration of sexuality, would never have won such applause, if there had been a true psychology. Psychoanalysis —by which term one ought to signify exclusively the system of Freud—has still many admirers to-day; it is indeed a theory quite after the heart of the materialist, and it cannot be accepted unless one is ready to accept its materialistic premises too.

It is mainly Freudian psychoanalysis which propagated in our days the idea of all love being originally and basically sexual. The fact that no trace of sexuality may be found either in maternal love or in the love between friends, does not trouble the psychoanalyst. But true psychology, intent first on considering the phenomena as they are, cannot ignore such facts. There is, of course, sexual love; but there is also sexual desire without any love, and there is love without any sexuality.

Adolescence is not only the age of the first manifestations of sexuality; it is very often also the age of the first true love. But love, being more than mere sexual longing, must spring from a source other than merely the physiology of the sex organs.

Even in the mind of the adolescents, much as they may be impressed by the crude manifestations of sexuality, there is more than a mere desire for lust or for the pleasant sensations to be got from sexual experience. This something more than mere sexuality is indeed very dim, as a rule, and but little recognized in its true nature. The purely sexual longings are much more impressive, and seem to overshadow completely the other factors.

The adolescent mind is just awakening to the full consciousness of personality; it cannot but feel that human nature is not completely represented by only one of the sexes. Without any philosophy, the human mind knows somehow that human nature is complete only in both sexes taken together. The modern psychology of evolution speaks of a "longing for completion." This longing is not sexual as such, though it may find its expression in sexual longing and in the inclination towards the other sex.

This longing for completion becomes particularly strong in adolescence, not only because of the emergence of the

somatic substratum, bodily sexuality, but also because of
the state of uncertainty which the adolescent mind is ex-
periencing. Everything which promises alleviation of this
uncertainty, which seems to afford some hold in the ever-
changing outer and inner world, which lets the person
hope for an experience enhancing his feeling of personal
value, is welcome and desirable. Being capable of loving
and being loved, being even only of interest to a person
of the other sex, playing a rôle in another's life, is doubtless a fact which promises a strengthening of the consciousness of self-value and appears as an antidote for the uncertainty.

But this new experience partakes of the general ambiguity which characterizes nearly all sides of adolescent
mentality. The longing for completion, born of uncertainty and the striving for its alleviation, increases the uncertainty. The world of sexuality, and of all things more
or less directly connected therewith, gives rise to many and
formidable problems. It is a part of the new world disclosing itself to the eyes of the adolescent, and part also of
the new-born personality which as yet does not know and
cannot trust itself.

The problems are manifold. There are not only the unwonted sensations and cravings directly caused by sexuality, not only the disturbing feeling of something unknown arising within the very self, not only the awareness
of a force surging out of the depth of one's own being
and seemingly beyond all control of the self, a feeling
which sometimes gets so strong as to produce the impression of one's having fallen into the clutches of some strange

and uncanny power; there are furthermore all the new situations resulting from the changed attitude to persons of the other sex. The adolescent who perhaps has managed already to feel somehow sure of himself when in company with others of his own sex, is thrown back into uncertainty because of his desire to be recognized by the other sex. He or she is attracted by and at the same time recoils from the new situation. There is the desire for closer contact, mental and bodily, and at the same time a definite shyness. This shyness is due partly to uncertainty in face of the new problems and the lack of self-reliance, and partly to the nature of sexuality itself, which is not simply a longing for union but contains, however dimly, the knowledge that union means, in a way, giving up one's self. Even in the crudest form of merely sexual desire there is still a trace of this—that sexuality imports not only attaining satisfaction, but also giving something away. And there is in this vague and mostly rather unconscious awareness a definite foreboding that this giving away ultimately means giving away oneself. However, one cannot give away what one has not got; a person not feeling sure of being or having a true self cannot but recoil from any situation which would imply such a giving away of the self. A person, furthermore, who has just begun to get hold, so to say, of his self and is still not certain of his possession, cannot be expected to make a gift of this self, because he feels that nothing would be left to him, and that he would fall back into the state bordering on nothingness from which he has just recently, after long and painful struggles, emerged.

One way of escape is open to everyone who, bewildered by this "great and terrible world," looks out for some refuge wherein to dwell securely. This is the flight into imagination or into the realm of dreams. One who is dissatisfied with reality will imagine another world more pleasant, more like what he desires, more able to give what reality withholds; and a person dissatisfied with himself will be equally willing to withdraw into a world wherein he may see himself as he wishes to be—as a hero, as successful, as wealthy, as a lover, etc. Every situation which becomes difficult or impossible to face may cause such a flight into the unreality of dreams. The world of dreams affords not only the possibility of eliminating all unpleasant aspects of reality and of abolishing all obstacles; it is also a world which obeys, in every sense, the will of its creator. The dreamer is indeed omnipotent in a world of unreality. However unruly and exaggerated the desire for greatness may be, it can be satisfied in dreams.

Not all daydreams are dangerous and wrong. As long as they remain connected with reality and take account of the real conditions, daydreams may be quite useful; but we call them by another name—plans, projects of future actions, etc. The essential feature of the daydream, in the strict sense of the word, is its being remote from reality, its failure to consider the actual situation, its dealing with a behavior which will be realized either never at all, or only eventually in a far-off future. Imaginings which become fruitful because they are preparations for action are quite distinct from those which are entertained for the sake of evading reality. It would be wrong to condemn all dreaming without restriction; many a great deed has been born from dreams, and quite a few of the famous men of action made their life a realization of dreams. But these dreams were of reality, of achievements, and took account of the necessity of doing things; whereas the daydreams which help the person to withdraw from reality usually contain little of personal activity, of risk and of endeavor, but much of lucky circumstances, of a friendly fate tendering to outstretched longing hands the golden apples of happiness, greatness and renown. Golden apples, however, have always been won by personal exertion, by courage and by taking risks; they do not fall at the feet of those who want them, simply to be picked up. But this is the attitude of the dreamer; the dream overlooks and skips all preparations, all patient waiting, all the many and unsuccessful initial strivings; it places the dreamer in the situation of his desires, in a world called forth by a magic wand, and spares him all the opposition he would have to overcome were he living in reality instead of among the fleeting creatures of his own imagination.

Such dreams are not training for real life. They rather draw the dreamer farther and farther away from reality, and because of this they are dangerous. A certain amount of dreaming is probably normal; man will, from time to time, indulge in such phantasies without any danger for his general behavior resulting therefrom. The question is only how great a place in one's life the dreams occupy, and how far they interfere with real activity. In a certain sense, it is even a right of man, especially in his youth, to dream of a better world and a happier existence. One cannot, assuredly, deny to the unhappy and the troubled the consolation they find in imagination.

Finding himself surrounded by a reality he cannot understand and confronted by a future he cannot grasp, feeling himself furthermore a stranger within his own ego, the adolescent often turns with a fateful necessity to the world of dreams. The outer and inner situation which prompts such a flight into imagination persists for a long time; no wonder, then, that dreaming readily becomes a habit. There is a definite danger in this habit, because it so easily estranges the person from reality—not only during the dreaming itself, but also outside of it. He who lives rather in imagination than in reality misses more and more the opportunity of becoming acquainted with reality and of correcting thereby his dreams. The more he is lost in dreams, the less he understands reality; thus, he is thrown back on his dreams, to an ever increasing degree, because reality becomes gradually still more strange and incomprehensible. A vicious circle is established which, in some (happily not very frequent) cases, may end in alienating the person from reality altogether and in incapacitating him for all efficient work.

Instead of grappling with the hard facts of existence, the dreamer moves in a world which obeys his slightest wish; he can fulfill all his desires without paying any price for their attainment. Returning to reality, he discovers that things are there very different; he then easily loses courage, and relapses again into the dream world.

We must, of course, try to arouse a youngster whom we see being lost in dreams; it is quite true that he neglects his duties (for instance, in regard to school work), because he is dreaming. However, it will not be sufficient in many cases simply to tell him that he must not dream, but pay attention to what is said in class or to the work he has to do. It may well be the case that he is retiring into his dreams, because he feels unequal to the work he is asked to do—unequal at least to achieve the success therein for which his ambition clamors. Dreams are not more univocal in their genesis than other features of behavior; they are susceptible of several explanations. We shall have to find out in every individual case why dreams play such a preponderant rôle in the life of this yoongster, or eventually also of this adult.

The content of daydreams may vary very much. Many of them, though not all, are indeed of things sexual. The sexual longings, to which satisfaction is denied in reality, seek for it in imagination. To this extent there is no difference between daydreams turning on sexuality and those which picture the realization of some other longing. A boy may dream of being a world champion or of becoming President of the United States; a girl may dream of having the most fashionable dress, the greatest number of "dates," or of being a famous star. But there is still another relation of sexuality to daydreams.

Dreaming is very common with children. Even normal children will sometimes get wrapped up in daydreams, though not so often as the adult observer perhaps believes; their being lost somewhere does not mean necessarily that they are dreaming. Playing is not a dream but reality to the child; and if he is absorbed so much in a game that he does not listen to what others say, it is not because he is out of touch with reality; it is because his reality is not the same as that of the adults, and things important to the latter have no importance for the child. But every child is capable of building up dreams; some are more gifted in this way, and some less; some are more driven to indulge in dreams, some less, because of their circumstances being different. A child who is perfectly satisfied with his sur-roundings will generally be less addicted to dreaming than is one who feels himself not quite in harmony with the world around him.

Dreaming is very easy for children; their imagination is curiously vivid; the imagery created by it is very like reality. Modern psychology has discovered the so-called *eidetic* images, memory images which are much more rich in details and much more like reality than the average images observed in adult minds. The children indeed do not confuse, at least after a certain age, these images with reality; but they are capable of reproducing impressions or of producing new images without any difficulty and with-out needing for this any help from reality. It has often been noticed that a child may be quite content with a very little bit of reality, transforming it by its imagination into what-ever he wants. But the young child can even dispense with this little bit of reality; he can play at being this or that, of doing this or that, without any real element entering. When children grow older, they need more and more of reality; a boy of four or five years may just jump around and feel that he is riding a horse; some short time later, he will want something to represent the horse, be it but a simple stick. The creative power of imagination diminishes usually in later childhood and becomes gradually less strong. It has been said that children are poets and artists; this is, of course, true only in a limited sense, but it is true in so far as imagination is concerned.

Thus, the capacity of building up a world of imagination without any help, without even a scrap of reality to found this world upon, is lost or at least very much enfeebled already in an older child. It is markedly less developed in the average adolescent, though the faculty of eidetic imagery may persist in these years. But this faculty is now more reproductive than creative. Phantasies and dreams in later years need some real foundation for their existence.

The adolescent does not play any more with toys or substitutes for such. He can no longer get hold of a thing and transform it according to his desires. For building up a dream, he needs some reality to give, so to say, the necessary consistence to the dream. The dream has to replace reality; even though the dreamer remains perfectly aware of the unreality of his dream-world, he has to make it as like reality as possible. This may be achieved by introducing some element of reality into the dream.

But reality does not lend itself to be fashioned according to the desires of the dreaming mind; it is hard, and does not obey our wishes. There is but one part of reality over which we have immediate and, as it seems, unlimited power; that is the reality of ourselves. And this is the point where sexuality comes in. Sexual experiences are very real, they are always at hand, they may be evoked at the person's will. Sexuality, therefore, is the very element which may supply the necessary real substratum for dreams. This applies, be it said incidentally, also to many daydreams of adult persons, normal and neurotic.

From this an important conclusion may be drawn. Paradoxical though such a statement sounds, sexual daydreams are not necessarily sexual in the strictest sense of the word. That is, they may express in the language of sexuality longings and ideas which in themselves are not sexual. A longing for superiority may be couched, as it were, in the language of sexuality. A girl may dream of becoming the object of desire to many men, and the essential side of this dream may be her compensating for some sentiment of inferiority, though these dreams may be accompanied by definite sexual sensations and clad in a definitely sexual imagery. A boy may picture himself as a second Don Juan or a new Casanova, and express by such a dream, sexual though it is, mainly his desire for being a "man," confusing as many do "success" with women and true manliness, or perhaps using this aspect of adult masculine life as a symbol for all the rest that his idea of manliness implies.

These facts are of a definite importance in education. If they are neglected, the sexual behavior of an adolescent may be quite misunderstood, and our attempts at influencing him may prove quite fruitless because of their missing the point.

The relation between daydreams and sexuality which has just been alluded to causes often a vicious circle to become established. Daydreams afford satisfaction to sexual longings, and sexuality supplies a basis and a starting point for daydreams. Thus, daydreaming may further the development of bad sexual habits. Frequently, indeed, these habits spring, not immediately from an excessive sexual desire nor even from "weakness of will," but from the wish to withdraw into the pleasant world of dreams and to escape the unpleasantness of reality. In some and not so very rare cases, therefore, it may be more necessary to combat the tendency towards dreaming than to direct the attack against the sexual habits themselves.

The task of the educator does not become easier because of these facts. Daydreaming, whether about sex or other matters, is due to the desire of flight from reality. Flight is caused by the impression of danger, by the terror which the premonition of danger arouses. It is indeed difficult to make a person face a danger which he fears so much that he takes refuge in flight. But that is just what we want the adolescent to do, when we expect him to turn his back on the world of dreams and to feel at home in reality.

It is commonly said that, to counterbalance the allurements of sexuality, one has to divert the mind from them. This is quite true; but it is impossible to divert the mind from one thing without supplying something to which the mind may turn. And this other thing must be at least as fascinating as the first is. Herein lies the great difficulty of the tactics of diversion, which difficulty is increased markedly by the fact that there is nothing to allure a person in things which in truth scare him. The allurement of the dream-world, we must remember, is caused not only by the pleasure of sexual sensation, but also by the illusion of a life outside of the terrifying reality.

Thus, it becomes nearly impossible to discover, least of all at a moment's notice, some topic which will captivate the adolescent's mind sufficiently to outweigh sexuality.

Bodily exercise has been strongly recommended, more for physiological than for psychological reasons. Sometimes this method works all right, because bodily fatigue may overcome sexual excitement. But it is not always possible to have the adolescent fatigued to a sufficient degree, because this might lead to some physical damage, and because it often interferes with work. There are moreover cases in which bodily fatigue acts as a stimulant of sexual excitement. Fatigue will moreover, if it is kept within the limits prescribed by hygiene, last only a short time, and we cannot stretch it over a whole day. Though there are, of course, times and situations which are more favorable to the arising of sexual desires and the production of daydreams, there are none which exclude these things.

Sexual excitement is, after all, something quite normal; one cannot hope to extinguish sexuality. It would be much better if some way could be devised by which the right attitude towards these things becomes established.

This goal cannot be reached immediately. The sexual habits and the preoccupation with sexuality depend, as we have attempted to explain, on too many factors to be so easily dethroned. The first thing to do, as it seems, is to break down the habit of excessive subjectivism. The world of dreams is a merely subjective one, different from and antagonistic to reality. The more a person lives in touch with reality, and the more at home he is there, the less will he be tempted to withdraw into the dream-world. The idea of reality must be taken in its fullest sense, including not only tangible things and society and work and economics, but the world of truths and of values too. We ought to train our children in such a way that they shall become conscious of the fact that truth and value are realities or sides of reality. It is perhaps not quite to the point that we usually speak of "ideals," whenever we refer to morals. Moral laws are just as much laws of reality as those of physics are. We are told by philosophy, and believe this statement to be true, that every being is one, and true, and good. But it is a long way from the acceptance of this theoretical truth to its application in practice. It is, however, our task to inculcate the truths so intensely that they will be transformed into principles of action.

The adolescent, however, is simply not at home in reality. To make him feel so, one has to make reality homelike to him. We must try to divest reality of the note of being uncanny and dangerous. Or we must, which is perhaps more true, teach the adolescent how to face a world which, up to a certain degree, will never lose all of its threatening, uncanny, dangerous aspects. The idea that life is, after all, in its very depth an adventure ought to appeal to the youthful mind; that is, it will appeal if the natural courage of the normal adolescent has not been broken or undermined by mistakes made by education a long time before the troubles of adolescence set in.

The training for reality and for the acceptance of all its laws—comprising, as has been said, those of morals too—ought to be started long before the beginning of adolescence. There is, in truth, no such thing as the education in sexuality; one can only educate a human person. The moral attitudes needed for making resistance to temptation possible in the field of sexuality are the same as enable an individual to resist every other kind of temptation. Young people who have not already learned how to offer resistance to the many allurements of the world, will hardly be able to act in the right manner when sexual temptations arise. But people who have been denied all gratification of even their most legitimate desires will not behave better, but perhaps even worse. They encounter in the field of sexuality at least some means for gratifying certain of their desires—means which are moreover quite independent of the consent of other people, means over which they have absolute command. Children who have been subjected to an over-strict education are at least as prone to indulge in sexual satisfaction as are those who never learned to deny themselves anything. Here as everywhere, a just mean has to be observed.

Many of the difficulties of education in regard to sexual behavior have their roots in years when there was as yet no trace of sexuality. Educational measures, taken to counterbalance undesirable sexual habits, are often unsuccessful because they consider only the actual state of things and neglect to take account of the previous history. The older a person has become, the more necessary it is to envision the totality of his behavior, if one wants to understand any particular detail. Individuals become more and more differentiated as they grow up, and the circumstances of their lives too become more and more individualized. Children, individualities though they are, are still rather alike in the general lines of their behavior and reaction; one may very often predict with certainty how a child is going to react to certain environmental conditions. This prediction becomes more difficult, the further differentiation has proceeded. To influence an adolescent, one has to be well acquainted with his total personality, which demands a knowledge of his present state as well as his previous history.

There is one further factor which deserves to be mentioned. Adolescent mentality is characterized, as has been pointed out, by an attitude of revolt. But open revolt presupposes a good deal of courage, which however the adolescent lacks. He cannot, as a rule, display his revolutionary feelings. He therefore either becomes recalcitrant in little things, refuses to submit to rules of relatively small significance (for instance, by becoming unpunctual), or he shifts, as it were, his personal revolt to a general field, siding with a revolutionary party or at least sympathizing with it; otherwise he has to find ways of expressing his inner attitude in a way which enables him to escape immediate consequences. His revolt is, corresponding to his general mental make-up, often that of the coward. His behavior resembles in a way that of the minor employee who for fear of losing his job does not dare to remonstrate against what he regards as an injustice done him by the "boss," but who, after the latter has left, will utter threats and picture to himself what he would have said and done, if it were not for. . . .

The revolting spirit of the adolescent resents all kinds of restraint, whether imposed by the rules of common life in the family, or of the classroom, or of the law, or of God's own commandments. But there are very few laws and commandments one can ignore and contravene without risking some eventually disagreeable consequences. If one lies, one may be detected; a theft will be discovered; absence from church will be remarked; neglecting one's duties will be punished, etc. But disregarding the sixth commandment may be done without any risk. Disobedience to this commandment is the very course for the cowardly revolutionary. The adolescent, of course, is not aware of these things; he feels that he cannot resist, that the urge is too strong, the pleasure too alluring, the opportunity too easy to allow of resistance. He will often indeed put up a show of resistance; but whether this resistance is serious, is a question one will hardly be able to answer satisfactorily.

This does not, of course, imply the reproach of insincerity. All these things escape the consciousness of the adolescent. In case he tried to resist, he is fully convinced that he did his best and nevertheless succumbed. And it would be a pedagogical mistake to distrust him; subjectively at least he is probably telling the truth.

A chapter dealing with these questions might be expected to make some few remarks on the differences existing between the two sexes. Boy and girl are very much like each other in the first months or period of their life; they develop gradually personalities characterized by their individual properties and furthermore by those determined by their belonging to one or the other sex. This differentiation grows stronger with the years. It is already quite marked before adolescence; it is very clearly defined during this period. The differences cannot but involve also sexual behavior. It is, however, difficult to find out what are the original, essential properties of the male and the female experience and consequently behavior, and what is the effect of education, tradition, and custom. One cannot overlook the fact that many things which, a short time ago, were generally considered as definitely "unwomanly," and seemed to contradict the very essence of female nature, have not only come to be tolerated, but appear to-day as manifestations of this very female nature. One has to be very careful when using the word "unnaturalness." Things which we believe to contradict nature, often contradict but custom. We might refer to our earlier remarks on embarrassment; under certain circumstances embarrassment was once regarded as the right and natural behavior, whereas now it has come to be viewed as a defect. It is very instructive to compare the descriptions of behavior in novels of different ages; if you put side to side (say) the behavior of young people in Richardson's, Thackeray's and Somerset Maugham's works, you will immediately see the difference. Man has not changed, nor woman either; boys are still boys and girls are just girls; but the ways of expression, the language in which the ever alike things are couched, change.

These facts are but too often forgotten by those people who regard as right that only to which they are used. This kind of mental rigidity is frequently criticized by the younger generation, perhaps not without some justification. The older people ought to be a little more conscious of changing times and customs. And changes come quicker nowadays than ever before. No change introduced by time can indeed ever alter the eternal laws of truth and of good. But one ought not to confuse these laws with mere customs.

It may, however, be very difficult to determine whether some feature of behavior springs immediately from nature, or results from nature modified by custom. It is, therefore, by no means easy to discover what are the essential differences between the two sexes with regard to sexuality. That such differences exist cannot be doubted. Human nature being one, a unit of mind and body, the physiological peculiarities of the sexes necessarily have their counterpart in the mental side. This does not, however, signify that the mental features depend on the bodily as their causes. To hold such a view would amount to the shallowest materialism.

The differences of the sexes in regard to sexuality can no more be considered in separation from total personality than any other feature. It would be quite wrong to derive the characteristic properties of the sexes from their being sexually different. The differences in the sexual sphere are but partial manifestations of the differences of their respective natures. Sexual education, in so far as such exists at all, must not use different means with boys and with girls because sexuality affects them differently, but because personality is different in the one and the other.

The attitude towards things sexual entertained by each of the sexes depends in truth on the essential characteristics peculiar to each. There may be, though it is difficult to prove, some difference in their sexuality as such, but most of the differences that a comparative psychology of sex may discover are due to sexuality being the expression or manifestation of the variant natures of the sexes.

It is not, nor can it be, the task of these pages to give a theory, however superficial, of education in general. But the remarks made in the foregoing paragraphs may serve as an excuse for not entering into a detailed analysis of educational measures suited to boys and to girls.

Modern life shows a marked tendency towards levelling down many of the differences formerly held to be essential. We have not to discuss here the question whether this is an advantage or not. It is a fact which education must take into account, but it is surely not the most important factor in regard to sexual education. A much more important consideration is that there is a general attitude towards these things to-day which creates some serious difficulties in education. The prevailing tendency is one of a definite overrating of all things connected with sex. Nobody will deny that sex plays an enormous rôle in human life. But the recognition of this fact is far from an endorsement of the way in which sexual questions are treated in many discussions and publications. The popular literature, even if it is not at all "immoral," and even when it deals with these questions quite seriously and from a scientific point of view, has a definite influence on the public in general and on the general attitude towards all these problems and facts. The scientific literature, and even the rather pseudo-scientific which shoots up around the former, have but little immediate influence on the minds of the adolescents. They may be very greedy for sexual things, but they are generally little willing to read ponderous treatises or even short articles which discuss these things in a matter-of-fact manner. There are, of course, certain magazines which capitalize a rather impure interest, and which have quite a few assiduous readers even among the youngsters. But what influences the adolescents much more than those magazines or even pictures is the general attitude towards sexuality. This general mentality penetrates into fiction, into articles on personal life and on the "way to be happy"; the young people are told, in certain popular articles, that "repressing" their sexual longings will handicap them and render them inefficient; they hear the adults talk rather unrestrainedly of things sexual; they read in the newspapers stories of divorce and adultery, how this star of the screen world has been seen with that one, etc. Their imagination feeds on these materials, and this is not even the worst of it.

The most disastrous result is that they come to develop altogether mistaken ideas on the place held by sexuality in life, on the rights and wrongs of sexual behavior, and they are easily led to believe that the morals they are taught at home or in school are but the ideas of oldfashioned, narrowminded, unmodern, reactionary—and envious— people.

These well-known influences make the creation of a counterbalancing force indispensable. If we desire to imbue the minds of our adolescents with right ideas on sexuality, we shall have to find means of exposing all these pseudo-scientific statements and to make the young folk see how mistaken are the views reflected in the magazine stories and similar types of literature.

In regard to this matter also, the thesis already presented must be repeated: there is no other way of revealing truth than by reason. Sexual education cannot dispense with reasoning, and reasoning, to be effective, demands that reason shall have been trained, and that it is held in the esteem which it merits. We shall not repeat here what has been said on this point in a previous chapter; but it must be emphasized, and it cannot indeed be emphasized too often, that the disregarding of reason, the appeal to "irrational" powers, and all the other equally shallow and dangerous catchwords of a pseudo-philosophy and pseudo-psychology, are in truth the greatest obstacles to an efficient education. And nowhere in education do the evil consequences of an anti-intellectual mentality become more apparent than in the field of sexual training. Superficial and imperfect knowledge, scorn of reason and its achievements, decay of morality, weakening of the public spirit, all these things which are so manifestly symptoms of our times are closely interrelated. But the root of the evil is doubtless the incapacity or the unwillingness of the many to understand and to appreciate the enormous importance of reason —of right reason which, Aquinas says, is the basis of all moral behavior.

Three things must be accomplished: the adolescent must develop a true idea of the rôle played by sexuality in human life; he must become aware of its place in the objective order of values; he must learn how to behave in the case of sexual temptation and in face of situations implying a sexual note in general.

The first task cannot well be detached from a general

instruction on human nature. It is the duty of our schools, and of all agencies imparting knowledge to youngsters, to indicate the right ideas. The materialistic views which represent man as but one organism among millions of others must be eliminated altogether. This ought not to prove too difficult a task; there are enough facts which plainly contradict these absurd ideas — for example, the fact of history, since no animal ever had history, nor will it ever have one. But nonsensical though these materialistic ideas are, they are still believed by many, they are taught in the schools, they are spread by lectures, by articles, by pamphlets, by books; they surreptitiously creep out of the pages of an apparently harmless novel; they are everywhere. They are praised as the most modern, most up-to-date views, whereas they are in truth stale derelicts of a dying time. But as the Emperor Julian the Apostate fervently believed in the pagan gods when their temples were already falling into decay or being transformed into Christian churches, so the high-priests of materialism cling to their obsolete and discredited creed. They do so the more easily, the less they are prompted by any true spirit of philosophy. They have learned to study, but not to think. "Knowledge comes but wisdom lingers." They have one formidable weapon: they are hostile to tradition, they are ever for the newest, the latest, the most modern ideas; they are reformers and, as such, akin to the revolutionary. Because of this they easily impress the adolescent mind.

This general spirit is the enemy. It is not necessary for such writers to state their theories in so many words. A textbook of physiology may not mention the problem of the rôle played by instincts in human life, and nevertheless by its general spirit influence the reader in a very undesirable manner. It is not enough to keep "immoral" literature from the young people; one has to be careful in regard to all kinds of reading. But it is impossible to restrict their reading to absolutely harmless books; they would tire reading them, and they would, and not unjustly, want to know more and to become acquainted with the other side too. One has, therefore, to prepare them so that they will not be harmed by these specious works. And, once again, there is but one way of preparing them: by the training of their reason.

It would be wrong to banish all information on the evil existing in this world, on the existence of so many who are blind to truth, and to deny to the adolescents all access to things which cannot but interest them and which they have a right to know. Ignorance is, moreover, no preparation at all, nor is it a protection. To beware of a danger one has to know it; unrecognized danger may become very attractive. It is our duty to point out that, important though sexuality is, it is nevertheless neither the most important side of human life nor the source of so many troubles as it is said to be by certain psychologies.

A true understanding of the rôle played by sexuality in human life cannot be obtained unless a true idea of the order of values in general is also inculcated. The reversal of the objective order of values which largely characterizes modern life proves to be exceedingly detrimental to sexual education. It is indeed difficult to make the adolescent understand that he has to refrain from sexual satisfaction and that he has to pursue higher values, when he is not aware of the existence and the dignity of these values. As long as the higher values of the intellectual, the cultural, the artistic, and the moral orders are held in scorn, as long as nobler and loftier sentiments are considered incompatible with the "modern" mentality, so long will there be but little hope of furnishing to the mind of the adolescent motives strong enough to make him desist from seeking unlawful satisfaction.

A certain laxity in the relations between both sexes which is often quite harmless, but which may easily degenerate into rather dangerous ways of behavior, is probably due also to the blindness to higher values with which the modern world is afflicted.

Because of all this, the third and most urgent task of sexual education becomes very difficult, more difficult than it ever has been heretofore. There is indeed scarcely any reason besides those implied in faith which could be pointed out to the adolescent as a motive for right behavior. There are indeed reasons which the human mind may discover even when it is not enlightened by faith; sexual morals are not as such "supernatural," they rest on the laws of human nature. But to prove this, rather subtle analyses and considerations are necessary which the adolescent will not understand and to which he will not listen. The help supplied by faith, however, may become rather precarious in the case of the adolescent. The attitude towards faith is, in the adolescent mind, not such as to afford a reliable basis to build upon. The process of reconstruction which involves the whole personality goes on likewise in the region of the soul (if this expression be permitted), where religiosity has its seat. The unsophisticated belief of the child must be developed into the conscious and reasoned attitude of the adult. Faith is, with the adolescents, something still growing and changing. The tendency towards revolt also becomes a serious obstacle, since arguments taken from faith rest on authority, and authority has lost much of its sanction.

Consequently, the problem of sexual education cannot and must not be separated from general education. Sexual behavior is but one feature among many others in which the basic attitudes of a person find their expression.

Some few words ought to be added on certain educational measures which are still applied, though they have happily become less frequent than they used to be. It is a serious mistake to threaten the adolescent with the bad consequences that his behavior in regard to sex will have in the future. The future, though it means more to the adolescent than to the child, is still something which is far away and of which there is no clear idea; the young people do not in general care overmuch for it. They will, moreover, sacrifice a still unknown future for a pleasant present. Such threats, if they are seriously considered at all, may aggravate a bad conscience; they may even become the root of rather serious mental worry, but they will become efficient motives only in exceptional cases. These threats are moreover based on mistaken and obsolete ideas. Sexual misbehavior does not become the cause either of mental or of bodily ailments (omitting, of course, the danger of infection). It is not permissible to make use of untrue statements, even with the best intentions. The young people are sure to find out that such threats are contradicted flatly by the assertions of medicine and psychology. Such threats are, furthermore, if believed, capable of producing a far-reaching discouragement; the adolescent, discovering that not even the knowledge of danger helps him in overcoming his longings, loses courage altogether, and having lost it feels that all resistance is useless. He, therefore, becomes less and less capable and less willing to oppose his cravings. Since he cannot help being what he is and acting as he does, he wants at least to get as much pleasure as possible.

Another point which deserves to be mentioned is the much-discussed question of sexual enlightenment. Since the writer has dealt with this matter elsewhere to a greater extent, some brief allusions must suffice. It ought to be emphasized that information on sexual problems must be reserved for private instruction. It is absolutely wrong to make such problems the topic of a course given to a class. Sex is a very personal problem; every individual has his own peculiar attitude, his own history, and his own difficulties. No general instruction can ever be capable of giving to the individual what he needs. Such an instruction has either to be so general that the adolescent will hardly know how to apply these things to his personal life, or it will have to enter into so many details that it becomes unintelligible, besides eventually wounding the feelings of some and thus reinforcing their attitude of revolt and reticence. The ideal situation would, of course, exist if the parents were capable of imparting the necessary information at the right time. But they are, unhappily, often neither capable of doing it, nor really willing, nor do they know enough of their children to recognize the opportunities and the needs. They have also but too often lost the confidence of their children. It is, therefore, very often the outsider who is much better suited. It may be a teacher, a priest, an older friend, a physician. The indispensable condition, however, is that a friendly and trusting attitude be first established. It is a great mistake to send a boy or a girl to a physician, even if he is known to them, for the sake of being informed on sexuality. The way for such instructions has to be prepared; they cannot be hurried.

CHAPTER VI

General and Vocational Guidance

MUCH HAS BEEN already said in the foregoing chapters
on questions of practical measures—on how to influence
the adolescent, how to get to know and to understand him.
It seems, however, advisable to reconsider the educational
measures so as to supply a clearer idea of the influence
which education may exercise. And it is necessary to add
some details on certain particular questions, among which
that of vocational guidance and vocational training is of
primary importance. This question deserves a special discussion because it indeed determines to a large extent the
future life of the individual entrusted to our care, and because it stands so much in the foreground of the debates
on education which are in progress to-day.

In following these debates, one easily gets the impression
that vocational training is the only aim of education. How
to develop the most efficient candidates for the jobs which
have been found to be the most promising, seems to be the
principal problem. The attitude of the defenders of this
kind of education is apparently this: academical training
is unnecessary and even dangerous; it is at best a super-
fluous ornament, but it has no practical value; the one
thing to do is to provide the youngsters with a most thorough professional training which will enable them to get
on in life, to find a job, to earn as much as possible. Now,

it is quite evident that all these objectives are very important. But it may be questioned whether they constitute education in the true sense of the word.

It seems that one ought to distinguish rather strictly
between education, on the one hand, and training, on the
other. Not all of education consists in training, nor is all
training rightly considered to be educational.

Education is primarily the formation of the whole personality; training is always concerned with certain faculties,
but seldom with the totality of the person. There are indeed
some kinds of training which involve several, perhaps
many, sides of human personality, and there are others
which involve but very few. But even the former are not
equivalent to education in the full sense of the term, because the all-round development of personality is not the
explicit aim of the training. Training aims at the development of a certain capacity for doing this or that—for being
a competent engineer, an efficient salesman, a good account-
ant, a hero of the baseball fans, etc. Or to put it in another
way, the aim of training is extrinsic to personality, whereas
education aims at personality itself.

Accordingly, no system of training can replace education. People who advocate so strongly the necessity of training seem to hold a rather optimistic view of human nature.
Apparently they believe that the development of character
or personality will automaticaly ensue, if the training is
of the right sort. Any special consideration of the faculties
not immediately concerned with the special training they
regard as unnecessary. Now, it is true that human nature is
one, and that it functions always as a whole. But this does

not amount to saying that in every activity all sides of human nature participate. As the training of the eye has no influence on the auditory capacity, and a good memory can co-exist with an underdeveloped imagination, similarly one side of personality may be perfectly trained without the others profiting very much or anything at all. Only a training which involves a large number of the separate faculties can be expected to be helpful to education.

This is the great danger of "vocational training," when it is made the very center and the all-important task of education. Human personality is complete and fully actualized only when as many sides as possible are developed. The defenders of vocational education wil refer to the fact that every training, if it is taken seriously and if consideration is not directed only to the purely technical side, involves a participation of many of the sides of personality; they will point out that every activity, especially one which brings the individual into contact with various sides of reality (as most jobs do), will necessarily tend to develop features of personality which are not directly implied by the special training. There is practically no occupation which does not demand honesty, a fine sense of duty, concentration, and other features which belong to character in general and are not exclusively concerned with any particular kind of work. All this is, of course, true; but it is very doubtful whether there is any one particular training which implies a development of all the features composing a moral character. Most of the special trainings seem to necessitate the development of some, but none of all, of the moral sides of personality.

It would be futile and nonsensical to deny the importance of vocational training. The specialization of modern culture has advanced too far to tolerate the neglect of special preparation. But complicated and specialized though modern life is, it cannot dispense with a thorough moral education. And such an education is not guaranteed by vocational training.

There is, moreover, a definite correlation between moral and intellectual development. The tendency which has been alluded to as characteristic of our time—viz., the scorn in which intellectuality is held by many—is of course in flat contradiction to any postulate of this kind. We shall, furthermore, be referred to the existence of moral personalities, who have had no intellectual training of any consequence. Such arguments, however, are not very convincing. None can deny the simple fact that even the good has to be known before it can become an aim of action; and human nature possesses, after all, but two kinds of knowledge—that which it gets through the senses, and that which is supplied by reason or intellect. The moral behavior of a person depends not only on his being willing to do the good, but also on his knowing what is good and what not. The more complicated the situations of daily life become, the more difficult is this knowledge to acquire, and the more urgent the necessity for a certain intellectual "training," if the knowledge is to be reliable. It is probably easier to lead a moral life when social conditions are simpler; the less simple they are, the more numerous become certain temptations, which are frequently not even recognized in their true nature. The more complicated life becomes, the less is it possible for an individual person to have a precise idea of the manifold sides with which he is in touch. These circumstances make man an easy prey for all kinds of phrases, slogans, and catchwords. He cannot but rely on authority; much though he may disapprove of it in general, he is nevertheless forced to accept it; but he generally does not even notice how far he is dependent on authorities whose reliability he is unable to test.

Only a good intellectual training will enable a man to detect the unproven assumptions, the hidden preconceived ideas, the basically wrong philosophy which underly most of the modern ideologies. Especially an adolescent who is going in for some work of a higher kind (be it teaching, or medicine, or economics, or what not) ought to be given a thorough intellectual training. All his moral strength, all his honesty, will not prevent him from succumbing to some "modern" ideas if they are presented to him, as so often they are, by enthusiastic defenders and well-trained spokesmen. Probity and the finest sense of duty, purity and a truly charitable heart, do not protect a naïve mind against the allurements of so-called progressive and modern theories. He who wishes to remain faithful to truth, must understand it thoroughly. But understanding is an intellectual achievement.

Education, therefore, has to provide—and nowhere more than in adolescence— an all-round development of character and a training of the intellect. Vocational education may not be neglected, but it is only a part of what has to be done.

Catholic education, more than any other, has to take all

these things into consideration. Just for the sake of being up-to-date and to compete with non-Catholic systems, it cannot neglect what it must conceive as its foremost duty—the development of moral character and the training of reason.

Human nature is one and a whole. One cannot separate reason from will, nor the development of the intellectual capacities from that of moral attitudes. Consequently, it is perhaps not beyond the scope of this work to say some few words on how the intellect should be trained.

In modern times there is a strong tendency to overrate the educational value of science. This tendency has its roots partly in the tradition of the eighteenth and nineteenth centuries, partly in the dominating rôle played by science in so many sides of modern life; engineering, economics, medicine, and many other types of work rest ultimately on scientific notions. The best way to prepare the mind of the adolescent for life and a good understanding of its problems is, therefore, believed to be a thorough teaching of science and, of course, of mathematics which is the sovereign instrument of science. It may, however, be doubted whether mathematics and science are really capable of giving to reason the general training which it needs. One must not forget that mathematical thinking is mainly formal thinking, even thinking in abstract symbols; it has its own strict rules which one has to master for achieving mathematical truth. But mathematics has no immediate relation to life or to reality. Not even science has such a relation in the degree it is generally supposed to possess. One must not confuse width of applicability with depth of penetration into reality. Science grasps but one side of reality, the side which lends itself to measurement and to expression by quantitative symbols. All that is quality escapes the grasp of science. And, as has been remarked already, science does not know anything, nor can it ever know anything, of ends and aims.

The humanities, on the other hand, have a closer relation to human life. It is not without reason that they bear their name, or that they were called in older times *"humaniora"* (the more human disciplines). Language is the great instrument by which men communicate with one another, by which they influence one another, by which they learn of their history and the deeds and ideas of past times. History, especially the history of ideas, teaches us to understand our own times a little better, and lets us discover the main springs from which human actions flow. So do literature and art. In modern times there is a strong prejudice against all the so-called "liberal" curriculum. The opposition to this kind of curriculum comes from overrating the efficiency of formal training as achieved by mathematics. It comes also, to a very large extent, from a mistaken idea of what is "practical." There is nothing, in truth, that is more practical than theory. Even if one does not go so far as G. K. Chesterton did when he declared that in a crisis one needs an "unpractical man," or at least a theoretician, one must concede that the great advances even of science have been achieved by those who were at home in the world of theory. The fact that something is theoretical and apparently far removed from practical aims, does not militate against its being very useful or even indispensable for practical achievements. There are certain facts indicating that the "humanistic" training may prove very valuable even for someone who is preparing for an occupation which is concerned mainly with science and with mathematics. Especially, all those who will eventually have to deal later on with people will definitely profit by having been trained according to a more humanistic or liberal curriculum.

These things need, of course, a much more thorough treatment than they can be given here. But it seemed necessary to allude to them because they are closely related to things which have to be discussed at some length.

Vocational training must be distinguished from vocational guidance. The efficiency of the latter is largely dependent on the influence we have been capable of gaining over the adolescent's mind, and on his own character and, of course, understanding. Vocational guidance is based on considerations of aptitude and of economic advisability. Aptitude comprises a rather large set of intrinsic factors; it is no simple quality, but a combination of bodily, intellectual, and moral factors. Though every work, if it is to be done in a satisfactory manner, needs some more or less special qualities, it is nevertheless always the achievement of a human person, who is an undivided and indivisible whole, and who therefore participates as such a whole in every kind of activity. An absolutely specialized vocational training is an altogether utopian idea. And so, too, is vocational guidance if it concerns itself only with the special gifts which enable a person to do this work or that.

Vocational guidance has to consider whether an individual is fitted for a definite kind of work, or to discover what kind of work might be best entrusted to this one person. The first question is whether inclination and aptitude correspond; the second question is to find out a suitable work for someone who either has no definite likings at all, or whose likings are not coupled with the necessary aptitude.

Children have, as a rule, quite definite ideas of what they would like to become; their ideas are of course childish, and for the most part are determined by merely accidental circumstances. Many things make a tremendous impression on children; certain persons are admired by them because of various reasons, and this admiration is extended also to the occupations they pursue. As they grow older, however, the children usually develop new ideas and give up those they cherished but a short time before. It is nevertheless quite remarkable how tenacious some of the childish ideas can be; they are known to be nonsensical or impractical, but they may still lurk in some corner of the mind. Many an adult will confess, half-ashamed and half-sentimentally, that he still occasionally thinks how fine it would have been to be this or that, just as he thought when a child of five years. To a certain extent, the case is the same with these ideas as it is with certain games; an adult will often, at least at certain moments, find pleasure in an absolutely childish game, and this not merely because of some sentimental remembrances but because of a curious pleasure which he gets out of the playing. But, tenacious though some of these ideas may prove, they are nevertheless recognized as being contrary to reason and to the demands of reality. Very rarely does a child know really what he would like to be, in so far as this is to be determined by his likings in later life. Only a very exceptional degree of talent becomes manifest already in childhood. Some famous mathematicians, composers and other artists are known to have shown their genius in or before puberty. Generally, however, the ideas which children have in regard to their future work are of no great importance. With adolescence setting in and the knowledge of reality becoming more comcrete, the purely imaginative choice of work has to be replaced by consideration based both on actual opportunities and on personal gifts. The adolescent, however, has but a very imcomplete knowledge of the world or of himself; and even this incomplete knowledge cannot be utilized because of its inconstancy. Many adolescents do not know, accordingly, whither to turn; many let their choice be determined by mere accident, by some job offered to them, by some opportunity which they or their elders believe they have discovered.

It is evident that the choice of work becomes much more difficult in periods of economic distress. To-day any youngster has to be glad if he gets any work, and he has often but little opportunity of choice. He has simply to take what is offered to him. On the other hand, this very difficulty in getting work may present an opportunity for a more careful preparation and a more conscientious choice. It is, of course, impossible to foresee whether an adolescent who, for the time being, can get no work, will be able to find at a later time the kind of work he is best fitted for. But this is no reason why he should not try to prepare for such work. The greater interval of preparatory time which is forced on him by the hard conditions of the present era, might be utilized for better equipment.

Vocational guidance has to advise the adolescent not only on what kind of work he is fitted to do and on the economical chances or risks, but also on how to prepare himself best for such work. This is especially true of all kinds of so-called higher work, for which the young people are prepared by college and university or other schools of equivalent rank.

Vocational guidance is desirable and even necessary, not only because the young people do not know enough of the real opportunities and the real demands, but also because they do not know enough of themselves. The leading idea of vocational guidance is, as is well known, to put "the right man in the right place." One has to find out for what work an individual is fitted, or what work is suited to him. Fitness depends on talent and on inclination. People generally work badly if they loathe their occupation, though loving it is no guarantee of efficiency. The relations between liking the work and efficiency are rather complicated. One person may be efficient because he likes his work very much, but another may come to like his work because he proves to be efficient at it. A work which a man at first liked may become tedious and even loathsome, if he is a failure at it and has to confess to himself that he lacks real capacity in this field. There is, thus, no reliable relation between inclination and capacity.

Many people feel attracted by some work they are quite unfitted to do. One has only to recall the great number of young people who want to become some kind of artist. Such wishes are very common in adolescence for several reasons. First, young people are impressed by the fame some artists have gained; the great publicity which especially screen actors enjoy fascinates the youthful mind. Young people are, of course, ignorant of the hardships, of the risks, of the great amount of hard work which artistic success entails. Another reason is that the adolescent mind has a natural affinity to art as a mode of expression; there are probably even in this prosaic age few youngsters who have not at some time indulged in artistic experiments. Poetry is still the most common form of artistic expression, because apparently it needs no special technique. Art has been often regarded — we shall not inquire with what right — as an activity linked especially to emotions. It is without doubt a mode of expression which enables a person to give vent to his feelings and emotional states. It implies, moreover, creation in a field rather apart from reality; it procures some intense satisfaction for the adolescent mind because of its being personal expression and creation and because it thus gives the illusion of an enhanced personal value.

These are reasons enough for the adolescent mind to feel attracted by the idea of art. The attraction is all the greater because the young mind feels that there is in art a part of reality he already understands, and in artistic creation a kind of work of which he already has a full knowledge. Although this is of course an illusion, it nevertheless contributes not a little to the adolescent's desire to choose art for his life's vocation. Now, everybody knows that true artistic gifts are rare, that true talent is not found in each of the many who believe they are talented, and that many foolish attempts to realize these vague dreams of a splendid future have ended in catastrophes, or at least in a serious loss of time and in deep disappointment. If proof were needed, this fact would supply it: inclination and even passionate desire are no guarantee of capacity. The contrary is likewise true; though the cases are much rarer, there are people who are definitely gifted for certain work and do not relish in the least the idea of having to do it.

The adolescent does not really know himself; and he cannot, therefore, know whether what he for the time being believes to be the very wish of his heart really corresponds to the deepest tendencies and attitudes of his personality. The inclinations of youth change as quickly as all other things in the adolescent personality. But if one were to tell a youngster that he is mistaken in his aim, that the work he has chosen is not suited to him, and that before long he will have changed his mind, one would supply a strong motive for his insisting on his choice. It is doubtless better to discuss the question with him in a matter-of-fact way, to explain all the objective sides of the problem, and to let the young mind draw its own conclusions. It is often quite easy to guess at the true reasons for his choice (e.g., opposition, admiration, love of "glamour," etc.), which have nothing at all to do with the fundamental issue. But it would be wrong to tell the adolescent bluntly that he is misled by accidental features. Even if he is ready for the moment to accept such an affirmation, he is sure to return before long to his views (or to replace them by similar and equally nonsensical ones), because his acquiescence in the criticism offered by a third person would entail the recognition of his own inferiority and uncertainty.

Opposition plays a rôle which is nearly as great as that of imitation. A child will often plan to follow his father's example, simply because he admires and loves him, and because he identifies the great place which his father occupies in his eyes and within the family with the work done by his father. But the child may also feel that he must choose a life quite different from that of his father. There may be no antagonism at all in this choice; quite on the contrary, the boy's decision may spring from admiration and from the feeling that it is impossible for him to become the equal of the person admired.

Prior to all decision regarding a particular job, however, a person who is preparing for his life's work must needs develop the right attitude towards work in general. The necessity of such an attitude is so obvious that one might almost dispense with its further discussion. It is, however, worth while to devote some consideration to the nature of this attitude and to the ways of engendering it in the adolescent mind. It may be well also to say some few words on this matter, because the conception of work entertained by a great majority to-day is not quite in accordance with the general principles of truth.

Most people look at work either as a means of gaining their livelihood, and eventually of gleaning as many as possible of the pleasures which life affords; or they see in work the means of indulging in some of their inclinations. They know, of course, that man has to work, because else he will starve; the few who need not work or work any more, are so rare exceptions that they may be disregarded. Quite a few of the latter feel that something is amiss with them, though they rarely care to find out what it is.

The attitude towards work must be based on a knowledge of what the real nature of work is. We cannot see the true nature of work merely in the fact that it furnishes the means of subsistence. Highly serious and important work may be done without any relation to subsistence, and very frequently there is an utter disproportion between the amount and the quality of the work done, on the one hand, and the living it helps to provide, on the other.

Work means, first of all, the production of values that last longer than the activity which produces them. This factor distinguishes basically work from play. Work deals with reality, and therefore implies responsibility; play carries no responsibility, because the fact of winning or losing, playing well or badly, has no influence on real life. Even if it is done by a man solitary and unaided, work implies always a relation to the community. Work is essentially an effort for others, or at least effort of a kind that others may profit by it; play considers others at the best as spectators, but it never produces anything which the others can, in some way or another, use. Work means, furthermore, obedience to rules and laws; this feature is common to work and play, especially games. But there is even here another great difference. The laws of work are laid down by reality; the material on which a man labors — whether it be a material in the strict sense of the term (like metal or wood), or an experimental undertaking in a laboratory, or the sounds a composer forms into a symphony — dictates to the worker. The rules of play are man-made, and can be changed whenever we like; the rules of a game are even, so to say, more man-made than the laws governing a state or society, because these latter laws, changed though they may be, are presumed to rest ultimately on laws of reality, on the essence of human nature, on the idea of right, etc.

It is, therefore, a great mistake to confuse play or games with work. In so far as games teach man to obey rules and to serve for the sake of an impersonal aim, they may be helpful as a training for the life of work. It is, however, not sure that this effect will be always achieved. A man need not submit to the rules of a game indefinitely and without any hope of ever seeing things changed, because he may leave the game at any moment. However, he cannot leave reality; he may walk off from the playground never to return there, but he cannot walk away from the actualities of life. While very few, if any, of our contemporaries reflect on this, there is no doubt that they sense the situation somehow; and there can be no doubt either that this factor makes an enormous difference in their acquiescent attitude towards the rules of a game. Games and play are, after all, synonymous terms.

It is always dangerous to take too seriously things which are in truth unimportant. By laying too much stress on games, one risks blurring the distinctions between reality and play. Games may prove in many cases an efficient means for developing a sense of obligation towards a group; it is not sure, however, that every participant will be capable of translating, as it were, the feeling of obligation towards his "team" into the necessary sense of duty towards the community. Nor is it generally true that features of character developed on the playground will, so to say, automatically become generalized and constitute integral sides of the personality, in so far as one is a member of society and of the "working front of mankind."

Play is essentially different from reality. It is not without a deep significance that the play of the child, activity on the playground, the achievement of the actor on the stage, and the playing at cards are all described by the same word. The play-actor may be a hero on the stage, and a coward in private life. The champion athlete may likewise be a coward in civil life. A man may utterly despise cheating at cards, and yet not mind employing very doubtful methods in business. There have been members of teams who were absolutely loyal to their comrades and crooks outside the playground.

The essential differences between play of whatever kind and reality have been overlooked but too commonly. This oversight has led to a general overrating of the educational values of sports and games. That such educational value exists, cannot be challenged, but one might well question whether it is as great as it is commonly believed to be. This common opinion rests on a mistaken assumption, of which the enthusiastic defenders of education by athletics are quite unaware. The assumption is that attitudes which seem to be *formally* just the same are also necessarily the same *materially*. On the contrary, an apparently identical feature of character may receive a different signification from the different objects to which it is related. For example, honesty may be, of course, a general feature of character, which comes into play whenever a decision between right and wrong must be made; but honesty may be also limited to special cases. One need only refer to the very common fact that a man may avoid meticulously all dishonesty in business or in social intercourse with his friends, but may not mind in the least deceiving these same friends when a so-called love affair is in question. We shall see presently that the "same" feature of behavior may be morally good or morally wrong according to the object in question. For the moment, there is but one conclusion which imposes itself, namely, that the developing of a certain feature of character under special conditions does not guarantee this feature becoming a general one.

The idea that honesty, or courage, or reliability, or, of course, any other feature of character is always the *same* thing regardless of the objective situation, is an offspring of the relativism and subjectivism which were so dominant in the nineteenth century. Because the notion of objective values had been lost, and because morality was regarded as originating merely in subjective attitudes and moods, the objective side of situations, in which man has to choose and to decide, came to be neglected altogether. But it is, in truth, impossible to detach the subjective side of behavior from the objective situation conditioning it. To understand human behavior, one has always to consider both sides — the subjective moods, motivations, attitudes, volitions, etc., and the objective situation. A mere subjectivistic way of viewing behavior is as wrong as a so-called objective one

— the kind which the behavioristic school envisions; both sides belong together, and must not be separated. This point of view has a particular importance in education.

Vocational guidance is generally understood as a method devised for helping people to discover the right kind of work. It ought to be viewed in a broader sense, namely, as an educational influence towards developing the true idea of vocation. Vocation means being called to do a definite thing; but, for this, man has first to be ready to do something, not for himself, but for the community. He can, in fact, do things for himself only by doing them for the community; he is bound to belong to a community and to depend on it *materially*, because he can gain his living only by becoming useful to others, and because he needs even in the most elementary work the coöperation of others (for instance, for getting the necessary tools), and *formally*, because man becomes a personality only by contact with his fellows. The true meaning of work has to be grasped first; the special problem of deciding in favor of a particular job will then become less arduous.

The development of the right attitude towards work is equivalent to the development of a right understanding of responsibility. The adolescent is as yet far from possessing a real conception of responsibility. He is unable as yet to feel as a member of a community; being such a member means, in fact, being the equal (at least *qua* member) of all the other members. But the community consists largely — and, in so far as work is concerned, almost exclusively — of adults. Though fully aware that he is developing into an adult, the adolescent recognizes that he has not yet attained this status; he does not fit in, because he is not sure of himself and, therefore, not sure of possessing the same status as the rest. His attitude towards work, like many of his other attitudes, is dictated to a great extent by his desire for superiority; it is, accordingly, very egotistic. The idea of work as a social duty generally does not appeal to him.

The adolescent is not, indeed, anti-social. In some of his moods he may behave as if he were so; he may refuse to join a particular set, usually that which his parents would have him choose, but he is not an isolationist by principle. He belongs, generally at least, to some kind of community. There is a set of youngsters of which he is part — the sporting club of which he is a member, the classroom, etc. But these communities are of a rather special character; they are limited, shut in within definite boundaries; they pursue, if any, only very limited aims. They are related to the true community of society, of the nation, of humanity, much as the adolescent's personality is to that of the adult man. These communities are intermediary forms between the rather unstable groups to which children belong and the stable community constituted on the basis of citizenship, common work, and common duty. Such as they are, these social groups of adolescents have no immediate link uniting them to the larger community of the nation or of humanity.

The goal of humanity or society is too vague to impress the minds of the adolescents, who may even feel that there is a definite antagonism between their social groups and the world of the adults. The whole ideology of the so-called youth movement rests, partly at least, on this feeling that the social grouping among adolescents obeys laws which differ from those governing adult society. It is quite right that youth should associate with youth, but it is wrong to let the adolescents feel that they are a world apart, having their own laws and being independent of society as it exists outside their circles. Different though youth feels, it has to learn that it is after all but a period of transition, and that its full import is just this — to serve as an intermediary phase between childhood and adulthood, for it is always the mature form which gives meaning and importance to the immature and preparatory stages. There is no denying the peculiar charm of childhood and even of adolescence, though the adolescents themselves do much to make us overlook the more pleasant sides of their personalities; but notwithstanding all the assets of the young we must bear in mind — and we must make the youngsters themselves aware of this — that maturity alone gives to an individual the full dignity of human nature. This does not, of course, mean that we ought to treat the adolescents as if they had no rights, as if they were nothing at all; quite to the contrary, we have to respect the dignity of human persons even in the undeveloped shape of adolescence, and especially to forbear from adding to the discouragement and uncertainty natural to this age.

Religious education may contribute much towards developing an understanding of social relations, and thereby an understanding of the nature of work. We may point to the glorious idea of the Mystical Body of Christ, an idea which the adolescent mind is quite capable of grasping, and which, when presented in the right manner, may even arouse not a little enthusiasm.

Enthusiasm is an attitude which the adolescent personality is very capable of assuming. It has been the common belief of past centuries that enthusiasm is a characteristic peculiarity of youth, and that remaining young is essentially equivalent to remaining capable of enthusiasm. Modern life, however, and certain rather widespread attitudes are adverse to enthusiasm. Too many people have suffered disappointments; too many who felt enthusiastic about certain ideals have seen these ideals fade and disintegrate; too many also are so fully occupied with meeting the daily difficulties that no room is left in their minds for enthusiastic interests. Youth, antagonistic though it feels towards the mentality of the older generation, is nevertheless very much influenced by it, and, in its desire to grow up, readily adopts some of the attitudes of its elders. Unfortunately, it is not always the best sides of adult behavior that are copied, and it is not always the most laudable adult habits that are cultivated. Enthusiasm has been decried as in conflict with modern life, which is said to be hard and practical and sober and full of bitterness. Enthusiasm leads to nothing; it is much better to work on, to push ahead, to battle for a better life, seriously, furiously, grinding our teeth and using our elbows. What is the use of enthusiasm, and what is there to be enthusiastic about? The general mentality of the nineteenth century, its materialistic philosophy and psychology (which taught people that values are but subjective means for satisfying desires and that these desires are nothing lofty and ideal, but mere transformations of vital cravings), the tendency to look at things "from below" — all these features of the past century could not but work towards a destruction of enthusiasm.

It is perhaps a symptom of this general process that certain words which originally had in truth a lofty meaning, and were intended to express fine and rare sentiments, have come to be applied to most trivial and insignificant things. Love is a fine word; but it is not used in its right and original meaning if, when asked whether he will have a drink, a person answers: "I would love to." The often criticized habit of using exaggerated expressions where they do not belong at all, finding unimportant things (which are disagreeable at most) "terrible" (though in the whole thing there is no trace of terror), or "tremendous" (though nobody would think of trembling), or "adorable" (though there was never a man who on such an occasion would fall on his knees and adore) — all this truly nonsensical custom became possible and developed only because the true feeling for things and their values had been lost. This habit is the reverse of sentimentality, but it has (as apparently contradictory attitudes often have) the same effect. Sentimentality displays an unjustified intensity of emotional reactions when there is in truth no reason for such a display, and therefore levels down these reactions; he who uses up all his emotional energy in insignificant situations has none of it left when some serious fact arises to which response with a stronger emotion would seem called for. The sedate, unenthusiastic, sceptical — nay, even blasé and snobbish — manner which is so much cultivated to-day produces exactly the same effect; no proper emotional response is elicited any more, however "moving" a fact may be.

This altogether wrong and even immoral attitude is sometimes confused with Christian equanimity, from which it is as the poles apart. It is indeed absolutely pagan in its essence; it is the attitude of the pagan stoic philosopher who, for the sake of escaping the pains of life which spare nobody, denies the existence of anything worthy of an emotional reaction. Not as if our contemporaries were really capable of achieving a stoic indifference; they lose only the capacity for finer and loftier emotional reactions, but they retain fully the capacity for coarse and low sentiments; they are angry, bitter, envious, and jealous. It is only when the fact of enthusiasm is mentioned that they superciliously decry such a reaction as unbefitting a serious man who knows what the world is like.

Youth copies the adults. Adolescents have an extreme fear of appearing ridiculous; they are likewise afraid of showing their feelings; they are troubled by the intensity of their emotions which they do not understand. They fear the unknown forces which arise within their own personality. An attitude recommending unemotional behavior is, therefore, very welcome. The coldness, the lack of interest, the matter-of-fact attitude of our adolescents — all those characteristics which make it appear as if youth had lost many of the essential qualities which older times used to credit it with — are often not spontaneous manifestations of the true adolescent mind, but are artificially assumed as a means of defense. They are meant to shelter the sensitivity of youth, to build up a wall behind which the uncertain and troubled mind may hide and feel secure from being disturbed by the inner revolutions and by the threats of reality.

But the natural emotionality of youth has to seek for some outlet. It is not possible to suppress it altogether. And thus it comes to pass that a quite undue amount of emotional energy and of enthusiasm is expended on objects which in themselves are not worthy of such reactions. What, in bygone times, was enthusiasm for the great achievements of history and its heroes, has become an enthusiasm for screen stars and "thrillers." The interest for things of a higher nature, for culture and art, for poetry and intellectual endeavor, has degenerated into an interest for games. The champion boxer is better known than a great statesman, and the results of baseball games are more anxiously awaited than the most momentous decisions of Congress.

This state of things, bad though it is, need not become a cause for serious misgivings, if there were some hope that this attitude were but one which will pass away with adolescence. But this is not the case. Modern education sometimes boasts of having diminished the distance which used to separate the older and the younger generations; so far as this has been indeed achieved, it has been done not because the older generation has really learned to understand youth better and not because youth is better prepared for adult life, but because the older generation, in many a sense, has itself not developed to full maturity. It has been pointed out already that there is a marked amount of juvenilism in the world of to-day. How can we expect the adolescents to develop into normal, moral, efficient and mature minds, if the older people behave very much like adolescents?

The blindness to higher values, be they of art or of culture, of philosophy or of some other intellectual field, is definitely dangerous. The habit of being enthusiastic about things which in truth belong to the lower regions of value, blunts all sense of value. It is not unimportant whether an adolescent learns to appreciate true art or not; if he comes to believe — and the general mentality as well as the uncanny power of propaganda and publicity makes him believe it — that classical music is only for the "snobs" and "high-brows," he not only loses an opportunity of enlarging and enriching his personality, but his whole sense of values becomes perverted. If he feels that it is more important to know the newest "hit-song" than the great poets (not to mention the Classics), and that mystery stories are the only kind of literature worth reading, he remains not only intellectually uncultured, but he misses the important training in the appreciation of values one may get from these things.

It has been ascertained that at least a large majority of modern youth prefer "vocational training" to the Classics. Of course, they do; they cannot help feeling in this way, even if there arises sometimes in their minds a doubt whether their attitude is quite right. They live in a world of economic difficulties, of ruthless competition; they are told that gaining as much money as possible is the only true aim; too many of them are deprived of various pleasures they are fully entitled to, and therefore want to become as proficient as possible in the art of earning money quickly. There are, of course, other motives — the desire of independence, the wish not to cost the family anything more or even to contribute to the family budget, and other incentives of the kind. There is also the determination not to do any work which is not "useful," that is, not in immediate connection with the job. Some of the youngsters who perhaps have a liking for Classical and humanistic training will renounce it, because it means loss of time and because they think that they will have later the opportunity of catching up. In this hope they are generally mistaken; longings such as for higher culture have to be nourished if they are not to wither away. They may persist, but mostly in a very faint manner, just as a memory of youthful ideals; but there is no energy left for the pursuit of ideals; a job and the daily cares and pleasures have consumed all the surplus energy which had once been there.

This predominance of the practical and the vocational, this preference for a training which has a direct bearing on economically fruitful work, is not characteristic of American youth alone. The same mentality is found in totalitarian States, though the motivation for urging the adolescents into merely vocational lines is there somewhat different. This mentality is surely an effect of the general economic situation, but it is also a symptom of a weakening of the true understanding of values. The notion that we must for the present renounce all striving for higher cultural aims and devote ourselves exclusively to work which is "practical" — work directed immediately to the production of salable values, work "which pays" — is not without some serious danger. If this tendency should become general and last for a protracted period, who will then be left to rebuild culture and to take up the old and too long abandoned traditions?

Catholic education especially ought to be cautioned against yielding excessively to these modern tendencies. In a mind that is concerned exclusively with practical goals there is but little room left for any kind of ideal notions. The overgrowth of the ideology of efficiency threatens the development of those sides of personality by which religion is kept alive in the individual mind.

It is, moreover, doubtful whether we ought to give in to this desire of modern youth. The statistical fact of a preference shown for vocational training is not quite univocal or convincing; there might be several interpretations. A very thorough analysis is necessary before we can be sure of what the true roots of this attitude are. It would be definitely hasty to give up an old tradition which, after all, proved quite useful for so many centuries, merely because it is contrary to some "modern" ideas.

It is indeed not immaterial whether energy and enthusiasm are directed to this aim or to that one. The subjectivistic error, to which allusion has been made before, causes people to believe that enthusiasm is valuable as such. Frequently one may hear the remark that the object pursued by someone (whether an adolescent or an adult) is indeed quite futile, but at least he is so enthusiastic about it. However, nothing which is not a value in itself becomes such by having aroused enthusiasm. Quite to the contrary, enthusiasm for something bad becomes bad, and enthusiasm for something futile becomes futile. The capacity to get enthusiastic about things which represent only rather low values is a symptom of a general decline of the sense of values. Such a deteriorization may easily spread to other fields too, and this process may well end with a total loss of appreciation of all higher and the highest values.

This general mentality strengthens the attitude of sophistication and hypocritical indifference which adolescents often display towards their interests and inclinations. They are definitely ashamed of evincing any interest in things which are neither practical nor in accordance with the common opinion. Their minds are focussed on the material side only; how to make money, how to gain influence, how to play a leading rôle, etc., seems to them much more important than how to become useful and how to make the best use of their personal qualities. This becomes a rather grave hindrance to vocational guidance. A youngster may desire to study, to become a teacher, to do some special work, but he will not say so; he will even try to kill his inclination within himself, because he has come to think of it as nonsensical or as sentimental.

There is much talk of personality and its development. There are courses given on this topic. Boys are supposed to learn from these courses how to be impressive and sure of themselves, and how to acquire the necessary qualities for being successful; girls are told of "developing personality and charm." Personality has to be developed, and adolescents may be very much in need of some help therein. But their impelling idea is not that personality has to be developed because of its perfection (in the general sense of actualizing all their possibilities) and because of the common good; their idea is rather that personality has to be considered as a means, as a tool even, which one uses in the pursuit of success. Success is, however, conceived as being identical with acknowledgment by others. How to make an impression, how to gain "publicity," be it on however small a scale, is the important thing. As a man remarked when he heard of a youngster who wanted to study psychology: "Oh well, but there is not much publicity in that." This man reflected perfectly the general attitude.

It is this mentality of the older generation which contributes so much to spoiling youth and dispatching it on a way which the adolescents, left to themselves, would perhaps not choose. The ideal of manhood is not any more, to the mind of the adolescent, that of a man pursuing some higher goal with enthusiasm and energy, not that of one who believes in some mission, but of one who has attained success and a large income. The attitude is like that expressed by Pericles when talking of the great sculptor, Phidias: "Who would not admire Phidias, but who would like to be Phidias?" As to the mind of the old Greek a man doing menial work (be it that of the artist) belonged by this very fact to a lower class, so to the modern mind someone who does admirable work but does not earn an appreciable income may be quite a fine fellow, but not a man whom anyone would care to be like. A teacher! Of course, there must be teachers; but there is neither money nor publicity in teaching.

A definite curse has been laid by some evil spirit on the

world of to-day. Its effect is nowhere so baneful as in the education of adolescents. How are we who want to inculcate in young souls the thirst for the ideal, the aspiration for lofty things, the reverence of truth, the admiration of all that is good and holy — how are we to overcome the seduction exercised by the utterly materialistic, opportunistic, and hedonistic spirit pervading all modern life, public as well as private?

It is a truism that the general mentality is very much in need of reform. It is less obvious that such a reform can be brought about only if we are able to reform the individual minds. We are evidently moving in a vicious circle. Difficult though it may be, we must nevertheless try to break through this circle. There may be means of influencing the general mentality; that is, however, not the task of education, which deals with individuals. A group or a nation cannot be educated in the strict sense of the term; education, when spoken of in regard to a multitude of individuals, has but a metaphorical meaning. The one thing education can and must do is to exercise influence on individuals.

We have to combat in each individual the disastrous forces at work in the modern world. And we have to seize every opportunity the adolescents offer to us. Much would be already achieved if parents would refrain from dissuading such adolescents as are willing to become interested in some not purely "practical" work. We ought to beware of strengthening in adolescent minds the inclination for immediate success, for publicity, and for a large income. We ought not to tell them that they are crazy to feel interest in things in which "there is no money."

The task of influencing individuals can be achieved only if we study every individual entrusted to our care and try to discover the ways of approach suited to his personality and the means by which to influence him.

Much may be gained by even letting the adolescent know that we do consider him as an individual. Few things are more distasteful to the adolescent — and for that matter to older people — than to be regarded as a "case" or the representative of a "type." The adolescent's whole craving is to be a person, and consequently an individual, and as such distinguished from every other individual. But being a case or being classed as a type is the exact opposite of being credited with individuality. A behavior which looks definitely "typical" to the observer may be felt to be very personal by the subject; we may shock an adolescent profoundly by calling some of his reactions "so very typical." Maybe they are, but to him they are very personal expressions of his experiences.

Much is expected, by some pedagogues, from typology; we hear of introvert and extravert personalities, of integrated and disintegrated, of cyclothymic and schizothymic types, and of quite a few others. Tests have been devised for ascertaining the type an individual belongs to, and we are told that there are definite ways of dealing with a personality belonging to each of these types. Real personalities, however, are not sufficiently determined by the type they belong to — even if these types were clearly defined in every case, which in fact they are not. No real personality is exhaustively described by calling it by one of these names. Nor is the whole question of typology so far settled as to supply a reliable basis for educational endeavors. It is not at all sure whether these types are as constant as some will have them to be; it is quite possible, even probable, that the type may change in one person. By establishing the kind of type an individual belongs to, we get merely a very preliminary idea of his character; we know practically nothing about his real self. If one were to base education on typological theories, one would risk engaging in but another of the many "experiments" which have been tried in the last years, and which have proved anything but an asset to education.

Every pedagogue will, of course, profit by experience; when studying a new pupil he is sure to recall someone he is reminded of, a "case" like the one he has before him; he will know that he has been confronted by similar problems already more than once. But this is not the same attitude as that provoked by too great a trust in the "scientific" statements of typology. The pedagogue recalls an individual, or maybe several individuals, but not a type. It would be a mistake to tell the adolescent that he is the replica of someone we have known. Such a remark is sure to destroy all confidence, because it seems to imply that we do not regard the adolescent as an individual person. We may, however, try to explain to him that, notwithstanding the fact of every individual being absolutely unique, there are certain features which depend on general factors; we might point out to him that certain jobs tend to produce a certain uniformity, different though the personalities be; that there are national characters, and also traits of behavior depending on age and state of development; but we must abstain from making light of his problems by calling them typical. Even if we mean only to imply that we understand his position or his difficulty, it sounds to the ears of the adolescent like a disregarding of the fact of his being an individual.

Instead of making use of such a typifying terminology, it is better to tell the adolescent of the "case" we remember. One might, for instance, say: "I am not quite sure whether I grasp fully what you mean, but what you tell me reminds me of another youngster I knew" (and then proceed to tell the story). He will then either protest and declare that his case is quite different, or he will feel that he is indeed understood. In the second case all is well; in the first he will probably, for the sake of asserting his individuality, elaborate his statements a little more and thus help us in gaining a clearer idea of his views.

Whatever course we may choose to take, we must beware of hasty generalizations. Generalization is proper in science; it is wrong in art. But education like practical medicine is an art; neither the one nor the other can ever become absolutely "scientific," since they deal with individuals, whereas science deals with generalities. Though medicine has to rely on physiology, chemistry, pathology, etc., and education has to take account of the findings of psychology, anthropology, and maybe sociology, the one will never become biology and the other psychology. They will always, at least as long as their true meaning is understood, remain something like an art. A painter does not draw a picture of "the Indian"; he portrays an individual person, this one Indian man, even though he may call his picture by a general name. This, by the way, is the essential difference between a true work of art and the kind of "illustration" used in a textbook; art is always of the individual; the illustration may be a "general image" of which there exists in truth no original. Likewise, the poet does not create a type, but a person, though his play may be named "The Misanthrope." The pedagogue deals with an individual person, though he may discuss the problems related to "the adolescent." The physician writes, as a scientist, on a "case" of brain-tumor; but as a practitioner he has to take care of an individual suffering from such trouble. Every individual is new, unique, not comparable to any other. Education and training have, therefore, to be individualized in the extreme. There is never enough of individualization. The greatest mistake education can become guilty of is a strict adherence to one pattern.

Education is doomed the very moment it becomes the slave of one definite pattern, however "progressive" it may claim to be. One may, of course, develop a certain technique of education; many things pertaining to education may be learned and taught. But the essence of pedagogy is nothing one can learn by attending lectures, nothing that can be fully explained in textbooks. Educational influence is based on the personal relation between the educator and the educated. The adolescents may have, as indeed they do, many features in common; the basic attitude of uncertainty is present in each of them, though in different degrees and differently expressed. Notwithstanding this uniformity, we have to consider every boy and every girl as a new problem in regard to study and to guidance.

Adolescents are difficult, but they are promising too, especially if they are bright. Dullness of intellect is the greatest handicap in education, not only with respect to special training or to scholarly achievements, but also with respect to the formation of character. A dull person may be trained in an automatic manner; he can never really be educated, because he is incapable of perceiving adequately truths and values. The obstacles arising from intellectual underdevelopment ought to warn us not to neglect the importance of reason in the education of character.

Character depends mostly on will; but will in itself is blind unless enlightened by reason. Values, the goals of action, are not "felt" but seen; the mind does not grope in the dark, but may pursue its aims in the full light of reason. There is not much hope for a true education of character as long as reason is held in scorn. A theory of education which rests on the principles of Catholic philosophy would indeed contradict itself, were it to neglect the rôle played by reason. Value or goodness is a side of being, and being is the proper object of the intellect. Reason it is which discovers truth. It has been said unto man that he shall know the truth, and the truth shall make him free.

INDEX

Abstraction: an achievement of the intellectual faculty, 83.

Academic Training: unpopular today, 82; attacked by moderns, 144, 150. See also **Education**.

Achievement: often confused with success, 100.

Action: appeals to adolescent, 80.

Adolescence: consciousness of self the chief characteristic of, 15; essentially an age of problems, 15; uncertainty as basic feature, 16, 20, 36, 41, 100 sqq.; sees environment changing constantly, 16; growing sense of personality, 17; elusiveness of self in, 18; formation of definitive self real problem of, 19, 20, 62, 114; sexuality not central fact in, 20 sqq.; explanation of instability of behavior, 25, 33 sq.; not an alternation of introverted and extraverted phases, 25 sq.; introversion first indication of adolescence, 28; curiosity keen in adolescent mind, 28; basic quality of adolescent mentality, 29; introversion and extraversion in, 29; longing for independence and repugnance to blind obedience, 31; desire for confession, 32; feeling of responsibility for self, 33; secretiveness as a result of uncertainty, 33, 34; why adolescents often seem aggressive and lazy, 35; not essentially a period of unhappiness, 35; for adolescent the future has definite meaning, 36; ways of understanding and approach, 35 sqq.; authority one of greatest problems in education of adolescents, 38; uncertainty explains youths' peculiar perspective, 40; anxiety in, 41; process of compensation and over-compensation in, 41; close observation furnishes means of approach, 42; adolescents critical of older generation, 43, 47, 113; easy victims of relativism, 43, 61; attitude towards objective truth, 43; deadly in earnest about their passing views, 43; educator must gain confidence of, 44; cause of oscillations in mind, 45, 57; strained relations with parents, 45, 62; resent unasked for advice, 46; regard older generation as utterly different, 47, 113; understanding among adolescents based rather on subjective note, 48; effect of bad example on, 48; too personal an approach inadvisable, 48; usual cause of arrogance and conceit, 49; adolescent's interest in sport, 50, 85; every interest reveals something of character, 51; interest in moving pictures usually superficial, 54; standardized and superficial views obstacle to understanding, 55; trend towards sentimentality in, 56; inadvisable to seek to surprise adolescent mind, 56; insistence on authority may provoke stronger attitude of revolt, 56; undesirable traits often rudimentary forms of features unobjectionable in adults, 58; period of preparation and training, 58; stern rebuke not correct way of approach, 58; difficulty of understanding adolescents, 59; resent all display of sentiment and pity, 59; revolutionary and destructive ideas of, 62, 63; clash between personality and surroundings, 63; desire authority while revolting against traditional authority, 64; attraction of Totalitarianism, 66, 67; regard themselves as representatives of future, 66; affected by idealism, 67; more impressed by personalities then institutions, 68; must be taught necessity of authority, 68; not impressed by experience of older people, 73; proposal to abolish all distance between adolescent and educator, 73, 107, 168; dangers of exclusive association of adolescents with one another, 75; relations with their family, 75; need of authority and guidance, 76; misunderstandings with parents mostly caused by latter, 77; behavior greatly determined by emotions and moods, 78; accessible to rea-